Manhattan Review

Test Prep & Admissions Consulting

Turbocharge Your GMAT: Word Problems Guide

part of the 6th Edition Series

April 20th, 2016

☐ *Coverage of all Word Problems topics relevant for takers of the GMAT*

☐ *Intuitive and graphical explanations of concepts*

☐ *125+ GMAT-like practice questions*

   · *Great collection of 700+ level questions*

   · *Ample questions with Alternate Approaches*

☐ *Mapped according to the scope of the GMAT*

www.manhattanreview.com

©1999–2016 Manhattan Review. All Rights Reserved.

Copyright and Terms of Use

Copyright and Trademark

All materials herein (including names, terms, trademarks, designs, images, and graphics) are the property of Manhattan Review, except where otherwise noted. Except as permitted herein, no such material may be copied, reproduced, displayed or transmitted or otherwise used without the prior written permission of Manhattan Review. You are permitted to use material herein for your personal, noncommercial use, provided that you do not combine such material into a combination, collection, or compilation of material. If you have any questions regarding the use of the material, please contact Manhattan Review at info@manhattanreview.com.

This material may make reference to countries and persons. The use of such references is for hypothetical and demonstrative purposes only.

Terms of Use

By using this material, you acknowledge and agree to the terms of use contained herein.

No Warranties

This material is provided without warranty, either express or implied, including the implied warranties of merchantability, of fitness for a particular purpose and noninfringement. Manhattan Review does not warrant or make any representations regarding the use, accuracy or results of the use of this material. This material may make reference to other source materials. Manhattan Review is not responsible in any respect for the content of such other source materials, and disclaims all warranties and liabilities with respect to the other source materials.

Limitation on Liability

Manhattan Review shall not be responsible under any circumstances for any direct, indirect, special, punitive, or consequential damages ("Damages") that may arise from the use of this material. In addition, Manhattan Review does not guarantee the accuracy or completeness of its course materials, which are provided "as is" with no warranty, express or implied. Manhattan Review assumes no liability for any Damages from errors or omissions in the material, whether arising in contract, tort or otherwise.

GMAT is a registered trademark of the Graduate Management Admission Council.
GMAC does not endorse, nor is it affiliated in any way with, the owner of this product or any content herein.

10-Digit International Standard Book Number: (ISBN: 1-62926-062-2)
13-Digit International Standard Book Number: (ISBN: 978-1-62926-062-4)

Last updated on April 20th, 2016.

Manhattan Review, 275 Madison Avenue, Suite 1429, New York, NY 10016.
Phone: +1 (212) 316-2000. E-Mail: info@manhattanreview.com. Web: www.manhattanreview.com

About the Turbocharge your GMAT Series

The Turbocharge Your GMAT Series is carefully designed to be clear, comprehensive, and content-driven. Long regarded as the gold standard in GMAT prep worldwide, Manhattan Review's GMAT prep books offer professional GMAT instruction for dramatic score improvement. Now in its updated 6th edition, the full series is designed to provide GMAT test-takers with complete guidance for highly successful outcomes. As many students have discovered, Manhattan Review's GMAT books break down the different test sections in a coherent, concise, and accessible manner. We delve deeply into the content of every single testing area and zero in on exactly what you need to know to raise your score. The full series is comprised of 16 guides that cover concepts in mathematics and grammar from the most basic through the most advanced levels, making them a great study resource for all stages of GMAT preparation. Students who work through all of our books benefit from a substantial boost to their GMAT knowledge and develop a thorough and strategic approach to taking the GMAT.

- ☐ GMAT Math Essentials (ISBN: 978-1-62926-057-0)
- ☐ GMAT Number Properties Guide (ISBN: 978-1-62926-058-7)
- ☐ GMAT Arithmetic Guide (ISBN: 978-1-62926-059-4)
- ☐ GMAT Algebra Guide (ISBN: 978-1-62926-060-0)
- ☐ GMAT Geometry Guide (ISBN: 978-1-62926-061-7)
- ■ GMAT Word Problems Guide (ISBN: 978-1-62926-062-4)
- ☐ GMAT Sets & Statistics Guide (ISBN: 978-1-62926-063-1)
- ☐ GMAT Combinatorics & Probability Guide (ISBN: 978-1-62926-064-8)
- ☐ GMAT Data Sufficiency Guide (ISBN: 978-1-62926-065-5)
- ☐ GMAT Quantitative Question Bank (ISBN: 978-1-62926-066-2)
- ☐ GMAT Sentence Correction Guide (ISBN: 978-1-62926-067-9)
- ☐ GMAT Critical Reasoning Guide (ISBN: 978-1-62926-068-6)
- ☐ GMAT Reading Comprehension Guide (ISBN: 978-1-62926-069-3)
- ☐ GMAT Integrated Reasoning Guide (ISBN: 978-1-62926-070-9)
- ☐ GMAT Analytical Writing Guide (ISBN: 978-1-62926-071-6)
- ☐ GMAT Vocabulary Builder (ISBN: 978-1-62926-072-3)

About the Company

Manhattan Review's origin can be traced directly back to an Ivy League MBA classroom in 1999. While teaching advanced quantitative subjects to MBAs at Columbia Business School in New York City, Professor Dr. Joern Meissner developed a reputation for explaining complicated concepts in an understandable way. Remembering their own less-than-optimal experiences preparing for the GMAT, Prof. Meissner's students challenged him to assist their friends, who were frustrated with conventional GMAT preparation options. In response, Prof. Meissner created original lectures that focused on presenting GMAT content in a simplified and intelligible manner, a method vastly different from the voluminous memorization and so-called tricks commonly offered by others. The new approach immediately proved highly popular with GMAT students, inspiring the birth of Manhattan Review.

Since its founding, Manhattan Review has grown into a multi-national educational services firm, focusing on GMAT preparation, MBA admissions consulting, and application advisory services, with thousands of highly satisfied students all over the world. The original lectures have been continuously expanded and updated by the Manhattan Review team, an enthusiastic group of master GMAT professionals and senior academics. Our team ensures that Manhattan Review offers the most time-efficient and cost-effective preparation available for the GMAT. Please visit www.ManhattanReview.com for further details.

About the Founder

Professor Dr. Joern Meissner has more than 25 years of teaching experience at the graduate and undergraduate levels. He is the founder of Manhattan Review, a worldwide leader in test prep services, and he created the original lectures for its first GMAT preparation class. Prof. Meissner is a graduate of Columbia Business School in New York City, where he received a PhD in Management Science. He has since served on the faculties of prestigious business schools in the United Kingdom and Germany. He is a recognized authority in the areas of supply chain management, logistics, and pricing strategy. Prof. Meissner thoroughly enjoys his research, but he believes that grasping an idea is only half of the fun. Conveying knowledge to others is even more fulfilling. This philosophy was crucial to the establishment of Manhattan Review, and remains its most cherished principle.

                  © 1999–2016 Manhattan Review

The Advantages of Using Manhattan Review

▶ **Time efficiency and cost effectiveness.**

– For most people, the most limiting factor of test preparation is time.

– It takes significantly more teaching experience to prepare a student in less time.

– Our test preparation approach is tailored for busy professionals. We will teach you what you need to know in the least amount of time.

▶ **Our high-quality and dedicated instructors are committed to helping every student reach her/his goals.**

International Phone Numbers and Official Manhattan Review Websites

Manhattan Headquarters	+1-212-316-2000	www.manhattanreview.com
USA & Canada	+1-800-246-4600	www.manhattanreview.com
Argentina	+1-212-316-2000	www.review.com.ar
Australia	+61-3-9001-6618	www.manhattanreview.com
Austria	+43-720-115-549	www.review.at
Belgium	+32-2-808-5163	www.manhattanreview.be
Brazil	+1-212-316-2000	www.manhattanreview.com.br
Chile	+1-212-316-2000	www.manhattanreview.cl
China	+86-20-2910-1913	www.manhattanreview.cn
Czech Republic	+1-212-316-2000	www.review.cz
France	+33-1-8488-4204	www.review.fr
Germany	+49-89-3803-8856	www.review.de
Greece	+1-212-316-2000	www.review.com.gr
Hong Kong	+852-5808-2704	www.review.hk
Hungary	+1-212-316-2000	www.review.co.hu
India	+1-212-316-2000	www.review.in
Indonesia	+1-212-316-2000	www.manhattanreview.id
Ireland	+1-212-316-2000	www.gmat.ie
Italy	+39-06-9338-7617	www.manhattanreview.it
Japan	+81-3-4589-5125	www.manhattanreview.jp
Malaysia	+1-212-316-2000	www.review.my
Mexico	+1-212-316-2000	www.manhattanreview.mx
Netherlands	+31-20-808-4399	www.manhattanreview.nl
New Zealand	+1-212-316-2000	www.review.co.nz
Philippines	+1-212-316-2000	www.review.ph
Poland	+1-212-316-2000	www.review.pl
Portugal	+1-212-316-2000	www.review.pt
Qatar	+1-212-316-2000	www.review.qa
Russia	+1-212-316-2000	www.manhattanreview.ru
Singapore	+65-3158-2571	www.gmat.sg
South Africa	+1-212-316-2000	www.manhattanreview.co.za
South Korea	+1-212-316-2000	www.manhattanreview.kr
Sweden	+1-212-316-2000	www.gmat.se
Spain	+34-911-876-504	www.review.es
Switzerland	+41-435-080-991	www.review.ch
Taiwan	+1-212-316-2000	www.gmat.tw
Thailand	+66-6-0003-5529	www.manhattanreview.com
Turkey	+1-212-316-2000	www.review.com.tr
United Arab Emirates	+1-212-316-2000	www.manhattanreview.ae
United Kingdom	+44-20-7060-9800	www.manhattanreview.co.uk
Rest of World	+1-212-316-2000	www.manhattanreview.com

Contents

Chapter 1

Welcome

Dear Students,

Here at Manhattan Review, we constantly strive to provide you the best educational content for standardized test preparation. We make a tremendous effort to keep making things better and better for you. This is especially important with respect to an examination such as the GMAT. A typical GMAT aspirant is confused with so many test-prep options available. Your challenge is to choose a book or a tutor that prepares you for attaining your goal. We cannot say that we are one of the best; it is you who has to be the judge.

There are umpteen numbers of books on Quantitative Ability for GMAT preparation. What is so different about this book? The answer lies in its approach to deal with the questions. You will find many 700+ level of questions in the book. The book has a great collection of over 125+ GMAT-like questions.

Apart from books on 'Number Properties', 'Word Problem', 'Algebra', 'Arithmetic', 'Geometry', 'Permutation and Combination', and 'Sets and Statistics' which are solely dedicated to GMAT-QA-PS & DS, the book on 'GMAT-Math Essentials' is solely dedicated to develop your math fundamentals. Another publication 'GMAT Quantitative Ability Question Bank' boasts of a collection of 500 GMAT like questions.

The Manhattan Review's 'Word Problems' book is holistic and comprehensive in all respects. Should you have any comments or questions, please write to us at info@manhattanreview.com.

Happy Learning!

Professor Dr. Joern Meissner
& The Manhattan Review Team

© 1999–2016 Manhattan Review

Chapter 2

Concepts of Word Problems

2.1 Averages

The average of a set of numbers is a number expressing the central or typical value of the set. It is calculated as the ratio of the sum of the set of numbers and the number of terms in the set.

Thus, for a set of n numbers $x_1, x_2, x_3, \ldots x_n$, the average (arithmetic mean) is calculated as

$$\overline{x} = \frac{\text{Sum of the } n \text{ numbers}}{n} = \frac{x_1 + x_2 + x_3 + \cdots + x_n}{n}$$

Thus, we have:

Sum of the n numbers $= \overline{x} \times n$

Some important points:

- If a constant number k is added to or subtracted from each term of a set of numbers, the average of the set would also increase by k or decrease by k, respectively.

  Thus, we have:

  If the average of $x_1, x_2, x_3, \ldots x_n$ is $\overline{x}$, then we have:

  - Average of $x_1 + k, x_2 + k, x_3 + k, \ldots x_n + k$ is $\overline{x} + k$
  - Average of $x_1 - k, x_2 - k, x_3 - k, \ldots x_n - k$ is $\overline{x} - k$

- If each term of a set of numbers is multiplied by or divided by a constant number k, the average of the set would also be multiplied by k or divided by k, respectively.

  Thus, we have:

  If the average of $x_1, x_2, x_3, \ldots x_n$ is $\overline{x}$, then we have:

  - Average of $x_1 \times k, x_2 \times k, x_3 \times k, \ldots x_n \times k$ is $\overline{x} \times k$
  - Average of $\dfrac{x_1}{k}, \dfrac{x_2}{k}, \dfrac{x_3}{k}, \ldots \dfrac{x_n}{k}$ is $\dfrac{\overline{x}}{k}$

Weighted average:

If the average value of a set of n observations is x_n, the average value of a set of m observations is x_m, and so on, the combined average of all $(n + m + \ldots)$ observations is given as

$$\overline{x} = \frac{x_n \times n + x_m \times m + \ldots}{n + m + \ldots}$$

Let us take an example:

In a class of 5 students, 3 students scored 20 and 2 students scored 15 in a test. What is the average score of the class?

Simply speaking, the sum of the scores is $20 + 20 + 20 + 15 + 15 = 90$

Thus, the average score $= \dfrac{90}{5} = 18$

Using the concept of weighted average, we have:

Average score $= \dfrac{20 \times 3 + 15 \times 2}{3 + 2} = \dfrac{90}{5} = 18$

Additional rules:

- If n numbers having an average x_n, are added to an existing set of m numbers having an average x_m, we have:

Final average $=$ Initial average $+ \dfrac{n\,(x_n - x_m)}{m + n}$

Let us take an example:

The average of 4 numbers is 30. What is the new average if the numbers 66 and 64 are included in the set?

Explanation:

Initial total $= 4 \times 30 = 120$

Final total $= 120 + 66 + 64 = 250$

Thus, final average $= \dfrac{250}{6} = 41\dfrac{2}{3}$

Alternate approach:

The average of the two new numbers $= \dfrac{66 + 64}{2} = 65$

Using the relation above, we have:

Final average $= 30 + \dfrac{2\,(65 - 30)}{4 + 2} = 30 + \dfrac{2 \times 35}{6} = 30 + 11\dfrac{2}{3} = 41\dfrac{2}{3}$

Note: This approach offers a quick calculation for the difference between the initial and final average values.

- If n numbers having an average x_n, are removed from an existing set of m numbers having an average x_m, we have:

$$\text{Final average } = \text{ Initial average } - \frac{n\,(x_n - x_m)}{m - n}$$

Let us take an example:

Average of 6 numbers is 30. What is the new average if the numbers 24 and 26 are removed from the set?

Explanation:

Initial total = $6 \times 30 = 180$

Final total = $180 - 24 - 26 = 130$

Thus, final average = $\dfrac{130}{4} = 32\dfrac{1}{2}$

Alternate approach:

The average of the two numbers which are removed = $\dfrac{24 + 26}{2} = 25$

Using the relation above, we have:

$$\text{Final average } = 30 - \frac{2\,(25 - 30)}{6 - 2} = 30 - \left(-\frac{10}{4}\right) = 32\frac{1}{2}$$

- When a few incorrect numbers are taken while calculating the average, we have:

$$\text{Actual average} = \text{Incorrect average} + \frac{\text{Sum of correct terms} - \text{Sum of incorrect terms}}{\text{Total number of terms}}$$

Let us take an example:

The average of 10 numbers is 48. It was later found out that two numbers had been taken wrongly: 36 was taken as 54 and 46 was taken as 32. What is the actual average?

Explanation:

$$\text{Actual average } = 48 + \frac{(36 + 46) - (54 + 32)}{10} = 48 + \left(-\frac{6}{10}\right) = 47\frac{2}{5}$$

- When the average of a group changes as a result of one term being replaced by another, we have:

New term = Replaced term + (Increase in average × Number of terms)

Let us take an example:

The average of a group of 6 increases by 3 when 72 is replaced by another number. What is the value of the new number included in place of 72?

Explanation:

Let the new number be x and the initial average be y

Thus, initial total = $6y$ => Final total = $6y - 72 + x$

Thus, final average = $\dfrac{6y - 72 + x}{6}$

Thus, we have: $\dfrac{6y - 72 + x}{6} = 3 + y => 6y - 72 + x = 18 + 6y$

=> $x = 72 + 18 = 90$

Alternate approach:

Using the above relation:

Value of the new number = $72 + 3 \times 6 = 90$

2.2 Speed/Time/Distance

Speed refers to the rate of travel, or, in other words, the distance covered in unit time.

Thus, we have the basic rule:

$$\text{Speed } (S) = \frac{\text{Distance travelled } (D)}{\text{Time taken } (T)} => D = S \times T$$

A few important relations:

- If the ratio of speeds of two bodies, A and B, is $a : b$, the ratio of the times taken by A and B to cover the same distance d is $\dfrac{d}{a} : \dfrac{d}{b} = \dfrac{1}{a} : \dfrac{1}{b} = b : a$.

- If the ratio of speeds of A and B is $a : b$, the ratio of the distances travelled by them in the same time t is $t \times a : t \times b = a : b$.

- If the ratio of time of travel of A and B is $a : b$, the ratio of the distances travelled by them with the same speed s is $s \times a : s \times b = a : b$.

Let us take an example:

Walking at $\frac{3}{4}^{\text{th}}$ of his usual speed, a person reaches his destination 10 minutes late. What is the usual time he takes (had he travelled at his usual speed) to cover the same distance?

Explanation:

Let the usual time be x minutes.

In both situations, the distance covered is the same.

Thus, the ratio of time taken is the reciprocal of the ratio of distance.

Thus, assuming his usual speed to be s, we have:

$$\frac{\frac{3}{4}s}{s} = \frac{x}{x+10}$$

$$=> \frac{3}{4} = \frac{x}{x+10}$$

$$=> 3x + 30 = 4x => x = 30$$

Average Speed: If a man covers different distances at different speeds, the average speed is given by:

$$\text{Average Speed} = \frac{\text{Total Distance travelled}}{\text{Total Time taken}}$$

We have the possible scenarios:

- If d_1, d_2, $\ldots d_n$ are distances travelled, taking time t_1, t_2, $\ldots$ t_n respectively, we have:

$$\text{Average speed} = \frac{d_1 + d_2 + \cdots + d_n}{t_1 + t_2 + \cdots + t_n}$$

- If a body travels at speeds s_1, s_2, $\ldots$ s_n, for time t_1, t_2, $\ldots$ t_n respectively, we have:

$$\text{Average speed} = \frac{s_1 t_1 + s_2 t_2 + \cdots + s_n t_n}{t_1 + t_2 + \cdots + t_n}$$

  ○ If the time of travel is t in each case, we have:

$$\text{Average speed} = \frac{s_1 t + s_2 t + \cdots + s_n t}{t + t + \cdots + t} = \frac{s_1 + s_2 + \cdots + s_n}{n}$$

If $n = 2$, we have:

$$\text{Average speed} = \frac{s_1 + s_2}{2}$$

- If d_1, d_2, $\ldots d_n$ are distances travelled at speeds s_1, s_2, $\ldots$ s_n respectively, we have:

$$\text{Average speed} = \frac{d_1 + d_2 + \cdots + d_n}{\dfrac{d_1}{s_1} + \dfrac{d_2}{s_2} + \cdots + \dfrac{d_n}{s_n}}$$

  ○ If the same distance d is travelled at the above speeds, we have:

$$\text{Average speed} = \frac{d + d + \cdots + d}{\dfrac{d}{s_1} + \dfrac{d}{s_2} + \cdots + \dfrac{d}{s_n}} = \frac{n}{\dfrac{1}{s_1} + \dfrac{1}{s_2} + \cdots + \dfrac{1}{s_n}}$$

If $n = 2$, we have:

$$\text{Average speed} = \frac{2}{\dfrac{1}{s_1} + \dfrac{1}{s_2}} = \frac{2 s_1 s_2}{s_1 + s_2}$$

Let us take an example:

A man travels from City A to City B. If he covers the first half of the distance at 60 miles per hour and the remaining at 40 miles per hour, what is the average speed of the man?

How does the answer change if the man had covered the first half of the total time taken at 60 miles per hour and the remaining at 40 miles per hour?

Explanation:

Let the total distance be $2d$ miles.

Thus, he travelled d miles at 60 miles per hour and the remaining d miles at 40 miles per hour.

Thus, total time he took for the journey $= \dfrac{d}{60} + \dfrac{d}{40} = \dfrac{5d}{120} = \dfrac{d}{24}$ hours.

Thus, average speed $= \dfrac{2d}{\dfrac{d}{24}} = 48$ miles per hour.

Alternate approach 1:

We can assume any suitable value of the distance such that it is divisible by 60 and 40.

Let the distance for each case be 120 miles.

Thus, the man travelled 120 miles at 60 miles per hour and the remaining 120 miles at 40 miles per hour.

Thus, total time he took for the journey $= \dfrac{120}{60} + \dfrac{120}{40} = 5$ hours.

Total distance $= 120 + 120 = 240$ miles.

Thus, average speed $= \dfrac{240}{5} = 48$ miles per hour.

Alternate approach 2:

Using the relation given above, we have:

Average speed $= \dfrac{2s_1 s_2}{s_1 + s_2} = \dfrac{2 \times 60 \times 40}{60 + 40} = \dfrac{4800}{100} = 48$ miles per hour.

Looking at the second part of the problem:

Let the time he travelled at 60 miles per hour and 40 miles per hour be t hours each.

Thus, total distance $= 60t + 40t = 100t$ miles.

Total time $= t + t = 2t$ hours.

Thus, average speed $= \dfrac{100t}{2t} = 50$ miles per hour.

                              © 1999–2016 Manhattan Review

Alternate approach:

Using the relation given above, we have:

Average speed $= \dfrac{s_1 + s_2}{2} = \dfrac{60 + 40}{2} = 50$ miles per hour.

Stoppage Time: Let the distance covered by a body be d. The average speed of the body excluding stoppage time be s_e, and the average speed including stoppage time be s_i. We need to determine the average stoppage time per hour.

Time taken to cover the distance d had there been no stoppages $= \dfrac{d}{s_e} = t_e$

Actual time taken to cover the distance d since there were stoppages $= \dfrac{d}{s_i} = t_i$

Thus, total stoppage time during the journey $= t_i - t_e$

$$= \dfrac{d}{s_i} - \dfrac{d}{s_e} = t_s$$

Thus, stoppage time per hour

$$= \dfrac{t_s}{t_i} \times 60 = \dfrac{\dfrac{d}{s_i} - \dfrac{d}{s_e}}{\dfrac{d}{s_i}} \times 60$$

$$= \dfrac{s_e - s_i}{s_e} \times 60$$

Let us take an example:

A train maintains an average speed of 60 miles per hour while traveling between two cities A and B. However, since the train stops at multiple stations between the two cities, its average speed comes down to 40 miles per hour. What is the average stoppage time per hour?

Explanation:

We can assume a suitable distance so that it is divisible by 60 and 40.

Let the distance be 120 miles.

Time taken, assuming the train does not stop between the cities $= \dfrac{120}{60} = 2$ hours.

Actual time taken by the train (including stoppages) $= \dfrac{120}{40} = 3$ hours.

Thus, total stoppage time $= 3 - 2 = 1$ hour.

Thus, the train had a stoppage time of 1 hour in a total of 3 hours.

Thus, stoppage time per hour = $\frac{1}{3}$ hours = $\frac{1}{3} \times 60$ = 20 minutes.

Relative Speed: Relative speed refers to the speed of a moving body with respect to another moving body.

- If two bodies A and B move in the same direction with speeds S_A and S_B $(S_A > S_B)$, their relative speed is given as $(S_A - S_B)$

  If B is d distance ahead of A, time taken by A to catch up with B = $\dfrac{d}{S_A - S_B}$.

- If two bodies A and B are moving in opposite directions with speeds S_A and S_B $(S_A > S_B)$, their relative speed is given as $(S_A + S_B)$

  If A and B are separated by distance d, time taken for them to meet = $\dfrac{d}{S_A + S_B}$.

A few important points:

- Time taken by a body of length x to pass a stationary object of negligible length, such as a signal post or a pole or a stationary man equals the time taken by the body to cover a distance equaling its own length of x.

- Time taken by a body moving at speed S of length x to pass a moving object of negligible length, such as a man running at speed s equals $\left(\dfrac{x}{S - s}\right)$.

- Time taken by a body of length x to pass a stationary object of length y equals the time taken by the body to cover a distance of $(x + y)$.

Effective or Resultant Speed: Resultant speed refers to the speed of a body which moves in a moving medium.

Let the speed of a body without the effect of any medium be S and the speed of the medium itself be M.

Thus, we have:

- If the body travels against the flow of the medium (also known as 'Upstream motion' in the context of a man swimming/rowing against a flowing river):

  Resultant speed (Upstream) = $S - M = U$

- If the body travels with the flow of the medium (also known as 'Downstream motion' in the context of a man swimming/rowing along a flowing river):

Resultant speed (Downstream) = $S + M = D$

- Speed of the body without the effect of medium (also known as speed in 'Still water' in the context of a man swimming/rowing along a flowing river):

$$S = \frac{U + D}{2}$$

- Speed of the medium (or 'River' in the context of a man swimming/rowing along a flowing river):

$$M = \frac{D - U}{2}$$

The diagram depicting the situation of a man rowing in a river is shown below:

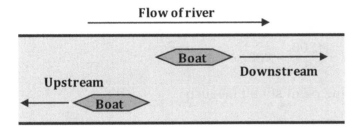

Circular track movement: If two objects P and Q move around a circular track of length L with speeds S_P and S_Q, we have the following relations:

- Time taken to meet anywhere on the track for the first time $(t) = \dfrac{L}{\text{Relative speed of P and Q}}$

- Time taken to meet at the starting point for the first time $(T) = \text{LCM}\left(\dfrac{L}{S_P}, \dfrac{L}{S_Q}\right)$

Let us take an example:

If P and Q move along a circular track of length 1200 meters with speeds 4 meters per second and 6 meters per second, determine:

- Time taken for them to meet on the track for the first time
- Time taken for them to meet at the starting point for the first time

Explanation:

To determine the time taken for P and Q to meet on the track, we need to determine their relative speed, for which we need to know their directions of motion.

Since their directions are not known, let us assume:

- **Same direction**: Relative speed = 6 − 4 = 2 meters per second.

  For them to meet again, Q has to cover one lap, i.e. 1200 meters more than what P covers in the same time.

  Thus, distance = 1200 meters => Time taken to meet = $\dfrac{1200}{2}$ = 600 seconds.

- **Opposite direction**: Relative speed = 6 + 4 = 10 meters per second.

  For them to meet again, P and Q together have to cover one lap, i.e. 1200 meters.

  Thus, distance = 1200 meters => Time taken to meet = $\dfrac{1200}{10}$ = 120 seconds.

To determine the time taken by P and Q to meet at the starting point for the first time, the directions of motion are not required.

Time taken by P to reach the starting point = $\dfrac{1200}{4}$ = 300 seconds.

Time taken by Q to reach the starting point = $\dfrac{1200}{6}$ = 200 seconds.

Thus, time taken by both to reach the starting point simultaneously

= LCM of 300 and 200 = 600 seconds.

Let us take a few additional examples:

(1) A man travels for 6 hours. He covers the first half of the distance at 20 miles per hour and the rest at 30 miles per hour. What is the total distance?

Explanation:

Let the distance be $2d$ miles.

Thus, total time taken = $\dfrac{d}{20} + \dfrac{d}{30} = \dfrac{d}{12}$ hours.

Thus, we have:

$\dfrac{d}{12} = 6 => d = 72$

Alternate approach:

Since the man covers equal distances at speeds of 20 miles per hour and 30 miles per hour, we have:

Average speed = $\dfrac{2 \times 20 \times 30}{20 + 30}$ = 24 miles per hour.

Total time of travel = 6 hours.

Thus, total distance covered = Average speed × Total distance = 24 × 6 = 144 miles.

Thus, one-way distance = $\dfrac{144}{2}$ = 72 miles.

(2) A person goes around the three sides of an equilateral triangle shaped field at speeds of 10, 12 and 20 miles per hour and reaches back to his starting point. What is his average speed during the journey?

Explanation:

Let us assume a suitable length of each side of the triangle so that it is divisible by 10, 12 and 20.

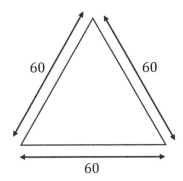

Let the distance be 60 miles.

Thus, time taken to cover the perimeter of the triangle

$= \dfrac{60}{10} + \dfrac{60}{12} + \dfrac{60}{20}$ = 14 hours.

Total distance = 3 × 60 = 180 miles.

Thus, average speed = $\dfrac{180}{14} = 12\dfrac{6}{7}$ miles per hour.

(3) A is twice as fast as B and B is thrice as fast as C. If C covers a distance in 54 minutes, how long will A take to cover the same distance?

Explanation:

We know that: B is thrice as fast as C.

Since C takes 54 minutes to cover a particular distance, time taken by B to cover the same distance

$$= \frac{54}{3} = 18 \text{ minutes}$$

We also know that: A is twice as fast as B.

Since B takes 18 minutes to cover a particular distance, time taken by A to cover the same distance

$$= \frac{18}{2} = 9 \text{ minutes}$$

(4) A man covers a certain distance between his house and office. If he travels at an average speed of 30 miles per hour, he is late by 10 minutes. However, if he travels at an average speed of 40 miles per hour, he reaches his office 5 minutes early. What is the distance between his house and office?

Explanation:

Let the distance be x miles.

Time taken to cover the distance at 30 miles per hour = $\frac{x}{30}$ hours.

Time taken to cover the distance at 40 miles per hour = $\frac{x}{40}$ hours.

Thus, time difference = $\frac{x}{30} - \frac{x}{40} = \frac{x}{120}$ hours.

Since the man was 10 minutes late in the first case and was 5 minutes early in the second, the time difference = $5 - (-10) = 15$ minutes = $\frac{1}{4}$ hour.

Thus, we have:

$$\frac{x}{120} = \frac{1}{4} => x = 30$$

For the above type of problems, we may remember a simple rule:

$$\text{Distance} = \frac{\text{Product of the speeds}}{\text{Difference of the speeds}} \times \text{Difference in time}$$

Thus, applying the above rule, we have:

$$\text{Distance} = \frac{30 \times 40}{40 - 30} \times \left(\frac{5}{60} - \left(\frac{10}{60} \right) \right) = \frac{1200}{10} \times \frac{15}{60} = 30$$

(5) A man covers a certain distance at his normal speed. Had he moved 3 miles per hour faster, he would have taken 40 minutes less to reach the destination. However, if he had moved 2 miles per hour slower, he would have taken 40 more minutes to reach the destination. What is the normal speed of the man?

Explanation:

$$\text{Distance} = \frac{\text{Product of the speeds}}{\text{Difference of the speeds}} \times \text{Difference in time}$$

Let the normal speed be S.

Case 1: New speed = $(S + 3)$.

$$\text{Distance} = \frac{S(S+3)}{(S+3) - S} \times \frac{40}{60} = \frac{2S(S+3)}{9} \dots \text{(i)}$$

Case 2: New speed = $(S - 2)$.

$$\text{Distance} = \frac{S(S-2)}{S - (S-2)} \times \frac{40}{60} = \frac{S(S-3)}{3} \dots \text{(ii)}$$

Thus, from (i) and (ii), we have:

$$\frac{2S(S+3)}{9} = \frac{S(S-3)}{3} => 2S + 6 = 3S - 9$$

$$=> S = 15$$

Alternate approach:

Let the distance be d miles and the normal speed be s miles per hour.

Thus, we have:

Case 1:

$$\frac{d}{s} - \frac{d}{s+3} = \frac{40}{60} => \frac{3d}{s(s+3)} = \frac{2}{3} \dots \text{(i)}$$

Case 2:

$$\frac{d}{s-2} - \frac{d}{s} = \frac{40}{60} => \frac{2d}{s(s-3)} = \frac{2}{3} \dots \text{(ii)}$$

From (i) and (ii), we have:

$$\frac{3d}{s(s+3)} = \frac{2d}{s(s-3)} => s = 15$$

(6) A man takes 8 hours to walk to a certain place and ride back. However, he could have taken 4 hours less if he had covered both ways by riding. How long would he have taken to walk both ways?

Explanation:

Walking time + Riding time = 8 hours

Riding time (both ways) = 8 − 4 = 4 hours.

=> Riding time (one way) = $\frac{4}{2}$ = 2 hours.

=> Walking time (one way) = 8 − 2 = 6 hours

Hence, walking time (both ways) = 6 + 6 = 12 hrs.

Alternate approach:

Two ways riding saves a time of 4 hours. It implies that one way riding takes 4 hours less than one-way walking. Thus, one-way walking takes 4 hours more than one way riding.

Thus, walking both ways will take 8 + 4 = 12 hours.

2.3 Time and Work

Let us look at the basic rules:

- If M_1 men do a work W_1 in D_1 days and M_2 equally efficient men do a work W_2 in D_2 days, we have:

$$\frac{M_1 D_1}{W_1} = \frac{M_2 D_2}{W_2}$$

Let us take an example:

If 20 men can complete a work in 10 days, how long would 40 men take to complete a work twice as large?

1 man would be able to complete the work in $20 \times 10 = 200$ days.

Hence, 40 men would complete the work in $\frac{200}{40} = 5$ days.

Thus, 40 men would complete double the work in $5 \times 2 = 10$ days.

Alternately, substituting the values in the above relation:

$$\frac{20 \times 10}{W} = \frac{40 \times D_2}{2W} => D_2 = 10$$

- If the number of hours (or days) required to complete a work is t, the fraction of the work completed in one hour (or one day) $= \frac{1}{t}$

For example: If A can do a work in 20 days, part of the work done in 1 day $= \frac{1}{20}$

- If the fraction of work completed in one hour (or one day) is f, the time taken to complete the entire work $= \frac{1}{f}$

For example: If A can complete $\frac{1}{4}$ of a work in 1 day, time taken by A to complete the entire work $= \frac{1}{\frac{1}{4}} = 4$ days

- If two men take x and y days to do the same work, the ratio of their efficiencies

$$= \frac{1}{x} : \frac{1}{y} = y : x$$

Let us take a few examples:

(1) A and B can do a piece of work in 15 days and 20 days, respectively. In how many days will they finish the work, if both of them work together?

Explanation:

Fraction of work completed by A in 1 day = $\dfrac{1}{15}$

Fraction of work completed by B in 1 day = $\dfrac{1}{20}$

Thus, the fraction of work completed by A and B together in 1 day = $\dfrac{1}{15} + \dfrac{1}{20} = \dfrac{7}{60}$

Thus, the time taken by them to complete the entire work = $\dfrac{1}{\frac{7}{60}} = \dfrac{60}{7} = 8\dfrac{4}{7}$ days.

Alternate approach:

In such questions, it is best to assume the total work to be the LCM of the number of days each person takes to complete the work (rather than working with fractions).

Let the work = LCM of 15 & 20 = 60 units.

Work completed by A in 1 day = $\dfrac{60}{15}$ = 4 units.

Work completed by B in 1 day = $\dfrac{60}{20}$ = 3 units.

Thus, the work completed by A and B together in 1 day = 4 + 3 = 7 units.

Hence, the number of days that both of them working together will take = $\dfrac{60}{7}$ = $8\dfrac{4}{7}$ days.

(2) A can complete a work in 24 days. B is 60% more efficient than A. What is the number of days it would take A and B to complete the same piece of work working together?

Explanation:

Let B take x days to complete the work.

Ratio of efficiency of A and B = 100 : 160

Thus, ratio of time taken by A and B = $\dfrac{1}{100} : \dfrac{1}{160} = 160 : 100 = 8 : 5$

Thus, we have:

$\dfrac{8}{5} = \dfrac{24}{x} => x = 15$

Let the total work = LCM of 15 and 24 = 120 units.

Thus, the work done by A per day = $\dfrac{120}{24} = 5$ units and work done by B per day = $\dfrac{120}{15} = 8$ units.

Thus, the total work done by A and B per day = 5 + 8 = 13 units.

Thus, the time taken = $\dfrac{120}{13} = 9\dfrac{1}{13}$ days.

Alternate approach:

Let the required time be t days.

Ratio of efficiency of A and B = 100 : 160

=> Ratio of efficiency of A and A-B together = 100 : (100 + 160) = 100 : 260

Thus, ratio of time taken by A and A-B together = $\dfrac{1}{100} : \dfrac{1}{260} = 260 : 100$

=> $\dfrac{260}{100} = \dfrac{24}{t}$

=> $t = 24 \times \dfrac{100}{260} = \dfrac{120}{13} = 9\dfrac{1}{13}$

(3) 2 men and 3 boys can do a piece of work in 10 days while 3 men and 2 boys can do the same work in 8 days. What is the ratio of efficiency of a man and a boy?

Explanation:

We know that:

$\dfrac{M_1 D_1}{W_1} = \dfrac{M_2 D_2}{W_2}$

The work in both cases is the same.

Also, we have:

$M_1 = (2 \text{ men} + 3 \text{ boys}), M_2 = (3 \text{ men} + 2 \text{ boys}), D_1 = 10 \text{ days}, D_2 = 8 \text{ days}$

$\Rightarrow (2 \text{ men} + 3 \text{ boys}) \times 10 = (3 \text{ men} + 2 \text{ boys}) \times 8$

$\Rightarrow 20 \text{ men} + 30 \text{ boys} = 24 \text{ men} + 16 \text{ boys}$

$\Rightarrow 4 \text{ men} = 14 \text{ boys}$

$\Rightarrow$ Ratio of efficiencies of a man and a boy $= \dfrac{14}{4} = \dfrac{7}{2}$

(4) A and B finish a work in t days. A alone takes $(t + 12)$ days and B alone takes $(t + 3)$ days What is the value of t?

Explanation:

Part of work done by A in 1 day $= \left(\dfrac{1}{t + 12}\right)$

Part of work done by B in 1 day $= \left(\dfrac{1}{t + 3}\right)$

Part of work done by A and B together in 1 day $= \left(\dfrac{1}{t}\right)$

Thus, we have:

$\dfrac{1}{t} = \dfrac{1}{t + 12} + \dfrac{1}{t + 3}$

$\Rightarrow \dfrac{1}{t} = \dfrac{2t + 15}{t^2 + 15t + 36}$

$\Rightarrow t^2 + 15t + 36 = 2t^2 + 15t$

$\Rightarrow t^2 = 36$

$\Rightarrow t = 6$

Pipes and cisterns: A pipe connected with a tank or a cistern or a reservoir that fills it is known as an inlet. Similarly, a pipe connected with a tank or a cistern or a reservoir, emptying it, is known as an outlet.

Let us take a few examples:

(1) A pipe can fill a tank in 3 hours. Because of a leak in the tank, it took 4 hours to fill. How long will it take for the leak to drain out the entire tank?

Explanation:

Let the capacity of the tank = LCM of 3 & 4 = 12 liters.

Quantity filled by the filling pipe per hour = $\dfrac{12}{3}$ = 4 liters.

Quantity filled by both in 1 hour = $\dfrac{12}{4}$ = 3 liters.

Hence, the leak empties 4 − 3 = 1 liter per hour.

Thus, the time taken by the leak to empty the tank = $\dfrac{12}{1}$ = 12 hours.

(2) A leak can empty a completely filled cistern in 4 hours. If a pipe, which admits 12 liters of water per hour is opened, the cistern is emptied in 6 hours. What is the capacity of the cistern?

Explanation:

Let the capacity of the cistern be x liters.

Since the leak can empty the cistern in 4 hours, the rate of emptying = $\dfrac{x}{4}$ liters per hour.

After the filling pipe, which fills at the rate of 12 liters per hour is opened, the effective rate of emptying = $\left(\dfrac{x}{4} - 12\right)$ liters per hour.

Thus, time, in hours, taken to empty the cistern

$$= \dfrac{x}{\dfrac{x}{4} - 12} = \dfrac{4x}{x - 48}$$

Thus, we have:

$$\dfrac{4x}{x - 48} = 6$$

$$\Rightarrow 4x = 6x - 288$$

$=> x = 144$

(3) Pipes P and Q are inlet pipes which can fill a tank in 3 hours and 5 hours, respectively. Pipe R is an outlet pipe. Starting with an empty cistern, if pipes P and Q are opened for 2 hours and 3 hours, respectively, and pipe R is opened for 4 hours, the entire cistern gets filled. What is the time taken by pipe R to empty the completely filled cistern?

Explanation:

Let the capacity of the tank be the LCM of the time taken by pipes P and Q

= LCM of 3 and 5 = 15 liters.

Thus, filling rate of pipe P per hour = $\dfrac{15}{3}$ = 5 liters per hour

Filling rate of pipe Q per hour = $\dfrac{15}{5}$ = 3 liters per hour

Let the emptying rate of pipe R = x liters per hour

We know that to fill the cistern, the pipes P, Q and R are opened for 2 hours, 3 hours and 4 hours, respectively.

Thus, we have:

$5 \times 2 + 3 \times 3 - x \times 4 = 15$

$=> x = 1$

Thus, the pipe R empties at the rate of 1 liter per hour.

Thus, time taken by pipe R to empty the cistern = $\dfrac{15}{1}$ = 15 hours.

© 1999-2016 Manhattan Review

2.4   Simple & Compound Interest

If a person borrows some amount of money for a certain time (T), then

- Principal (P) is the amount of money borrowed

- Interest (I) is the additional money to be paid

- Amount (A) is the sum of principal and interest

- Rate ($R\%$) is the interest that the borrower has to pay for every \$100 per year

Simple Interest: If the interest on a certain period is calculated only on the principal borrowed, it is Simple Interest.

Compound Interest: If the interest is calculated on the amount after each year (period) instead of only on the principal, it is Compound Interest.

The table below gives an example of how Simple Interest and Compound Interest operate. The principal at the beginning of 1st year is \$1000 and the rate of interest is 10% per annum. The details for 3 years are shown:

	Simple Interest				Compound Interest			
Year	Principal	Interest for the year	Cumulative interest	Amount	Principal	Interest for the year	Cumulative interest	Amount
1	1000	100	100	1100	1000	100	100	1100
2	1000	100	200	1200	1000	110	210	1210
3	1000	100	300	1300	1000	121	331	1331
	A few important points							
	The interest for every year (not cumulative interest) is a constant				The interest for every year increases by $R\%$ of the interest in the previous year			
	The amount every year increases by a constant value				The amount every year increases by $R\%$ of the interest in the previous year			
	$$I = \dfrac{P \times R \times T}{100}$$ $$A = P + I = P\left(1 + \dfrac{R \times T}{100}\right)$$				$$A = P\left(1 + \dfrac{R}{100}\right)^{T}$$ $$I = A - P = P\left\{\left(1 + \dfrac{R}{100}\right)^{T} - 1\right\}$$			

Concept of compounding: In compound interest, the interest need not always be collected annually. Interest may be collected semi-annually, quarterly, etc. In such cases, the formula for the amount under the compound interest is modified to:

$$A = P\left(1 + \frac{\frac{R}{n}}{100}\right)^{(T \times n)}$$

Here, n represents the number of compounding, for example: $n = 2$ implies compounding is done semi-annually, while $n = 4$ implies compounding is done quarterly.

Difference between Compound Interest and Simple Interest after 2 years:

Let us consider Principal P and Rate of interest $R\%$. The difference can be easily observed from the table below:

Year	Simple Interest for the year	Compound Interest for the year
1	$R\%$ of $P = x$	$R\%$ of $P = x$
2	$R\%$ of $P = x$	$(R\%$ of $P) + (R\%$ of $x) = x + R\%$ of x
Total	**$2x$**	**$2x + R\%$ of x**

Compound Interest and Simple Interest is the same for a certain sum of money at the same rate for the first year.

Difference after 2 years with interest calculated yearly:

Compound Interest – Simple Interest

$= R\%$ of $x = R\%$ of $(R\%$ of $P)$

$$= P\left(\frac{R}{100}\right)^2$$

Let us take a few examples:

(1) In how many years will a principal of \$400 yield an interest of \$100 given that the rate of interest and the number of years are numerically equal?

Explanation:

Let Rate of interest (%) = Time = k.

Since the principal (P) is \$400, we have:

Simple Interest $= \dfrac{P \times R \times T}{100}$

$\Rightarrow 100 = \dfrac{400 \times k \times k}{100}$

$\Rightarrow k = 25$

Thus, the required time is 25 years.

(2) In how many years at 10% simple interest per annum will the amount become 5 times the principal?

Explanation:

Since the amount becomes 5 times the principal, the interest accumulated must be 4 times the principal.

Let the principal be P and the time taken be T.

Thus, we have:

$$\frac{P \times 10 \times T}{100} = 4P$$

$$=> T = 40$$

(3) A sum of money invested under simple interest triples in 6 years. In how many years would the sum of money become 27 times its value?

What would be the answer if the sum of money was invested under compound interest?

Explanation:

Let the sum of money (Principal) be P.

Thus, the amount after 6 years = $3P$.

Thus, interest accumulated in 6 years = $3P - P = 2P$

Thus, for the interest to be $2P$, time taken is 6 years.

If the sum of money has to be 27 times, i.e. the amount is $27P$, interest accumulated $= 27P - P = 26P$

Thus, for the interest to be $26P$, time taken

$$= \frac{6}{2} \times 26 = 78 \text{ years.}$$

Thus, time taken is 78 years.

Let us now see the scenario under compound interest:

We know that the value of the sum becomes 3 times in 6 years.

Thus, we have:

P becomes $3P$ in 6 years

$=> 3P$ becomes $3 \times 3P = 9P$ in another 6 years, i.e. $6 + 6 = 12$ years

$=> 9P$ becomes $3 \times 9P = 27P$ in another 6 years, i.e. $12 + 6 = 18$ years.

Thus, the time taken is 18 years.

(4) A sum of money invested under simple interest amounts to $1500 after 5 years and $1600 after 7 years. What is the rate of interest?

Explanation:

Let the sum of money invested (Principal) be P.

Let the rate of interest be $R\%$.

Thus, amount after 5 years:

$P + \dfrac{5PR}{100} = 1500\ldots$ (i)

Amount after 7 years:

$P + \dfrac{7PR}{100} = 1600\ldots$ (ii)

From (ii) – (i):

$P\left(\dfrac{2R}{100}\right) = 100 => \dfrac{PR}{100} = 50\ldots$ (iii)

Substituting the above in (i):

$P + 5 \times 50 = 1500 => P = 1250$

Thus, from (iii):

$$\frac{1250 \times R}{100} = 50 => R = 4$$

Alternate approach:

The interest accumulated in $7 - 5 = 2$ years $= \$1600 - \$1500 = \$100$

Thus, interest accumulated each year $= \$\dfrac{100}{2} = \$50$

Thus, interest accumulated in 5 years $= \$ (5 \times 50) = \$250$

Thus, Principal $= \$1500 - \$250 = \$1250$

Thus, interest per year on $1250 is $50

$=>$ Rate of interest $= \dfrac{50}{1250} \times 100 = 4$

(5) A sum of money invested under compound interest gives $240 interest in the second year and $288 interest in the third year. What is the value of the sum invested?

Explanation:

We know that in compound interest, the interest for every year increases by $R\%$ of the interest in the previous year (where $R\%$ is the rate of interest).

Thus, percent increase in the interest from the second year to the third year

$$= \frac{288 - 240}{240} \times 100 = \frac{48}{240} \times 100 = 20\%$$

Thus, the percent increase in the interest from the first year to the second year is also 20%.

Thus, we have:

$(100 + 20)\% = 120\%$ of the Interest in the first year = Interest in the second year

$=> 120\%$ of the Interest in the first year $= \$240$

=> Interest in the first year = \$ $\left(\dfrac{240}{120} \times 100\right)$ = \$200

Since the first year interest is simply *R*% of the invested sum, we have:

20% of Invested sum = \$200

=> Invested sum of money = \$ $\left(\dfrac{200}{20} \times 100\right)$ = \$1000

In the GMAT, only two kinds of questions asked: Problem Solving and Data Sufficiency.

Problem Solving

Problem solving (PS) questions may not be new to you. You must have seen these types of questions in your school or college days. The format is as follows: There is a question stem and is followed by options, out of which, only one option is correct or is the best option that answers the question correctly.

PS questions measure your skill to solve numerical problems, interpret graphical data, and assess information. These questions present to you five options and no option is phrased as "None of these." Mostly the numeric options, unlike algebraic expressions, are presented in an ascending order from option A through E, occasionally in a descending order until there is a specific purpose not to do so.

Data Sufficiency

For most of you, Data Sufficiency (DS) may be a new format. The DS format is very unique to the GMAT exam. The format is as follows: There is a question stem followed by two statements, labeled statement (1) and statement (2). These statements contain additional information.

Your task is to use the additional information from each statement alone to answer the question. If none of the statements alone helps you answer the question, you must use the information from both the statements together. There may be questions which cannot be answered even after combining the additional information given in both the statements. Based on this, the question always follows standard five options which are always in a fixed order.

(A) Statement (1) ALONE is sufficient, but statement (2) ALONE is not sufficient to answer the question asked.

(B) Statement (2) ALONE is sufficient, but statement (1) ALONE is not sufficient to answer the question asked.

(C) BOTH statements (1) and (2) TOGETHER are sufficient to answer the question asked, but NEITHER statement ALONE is sufficient to answer the question asked.

(D) EACH statement ALONE is sufficient to answer the question asked.

(E) Statements (1) and (2) TOGETHER are NOT sufficient to answer the question asked, and additional data specific to the problem are needed.

In the next chapters, you will find 135 GMAT-like quants questions. Best of luck!

Chapter 3

Practice Questions

3.1   Problem Solving

1. Ann and Bob started traveling from City X at 12 noon. Ann walked till a lake that was between 2 miles and 3 miles, inclusive, from City X, and returned to City X between 1:30 pm and 1:45pm, inclusive. If Bob walked 3 miles farther than Ann and returned home at 4:00 pm, which of the following statements must be true?

   I.   The speed of Bob was greater than that of Ann.
   II. Ann's speed was between 2 and 3 miles per hour.
   III. The maximum speed of Ann is greater than the maximum speed of Bob.

   (A) Only I
   (B) Only II
   (C) Only III
   (D) Both II and III
   (E) I, II and III

   Solve yourself:

2. A man finds a stationary bus, at a distance of 500 feet, ahead of him and starts running towards it at a speed of 30 feet per second. After 10 seconds, the bus starts moving at a speed of 25 feet per second away from the man. After another 20 seconds, the bus speeds off at a speed of 100 feet per second. If the man kept running towards the bus throughout this time, what was the shortest distance between the man and the bus?

   (A) 50 feet
   (B) 100 feet
   (C) 150 feet
   (D) 200 feet
   (E) 300 feet

   Solve yourself:

3. Danny drove at an average speed of 60 miles per hour for some time and then at an average speed of 120 miles per hour for the rest of the journey. If he made no stops

during the trip and his average speed for the entire journey was 100 miles per hour, for what fraction of the total time did he drive at 60 miles per hour?

(A) $\dfrac{1}{5}$

(B) $\dfrac{1}{3}$

(C) $\dfrac{1}{2}$

(D) $\dfrac{2}{3}$

(E) $\dfrac{4}{5}$

Solve yourself:

4. A man drove from home at an average speed of 30 miles per hour to a rail station, from where he travelled by train to his office at an average speed of 60 miles per hour. If the entire distance, from his home to the office, was 150 miles and the entire trip took 3.5 hours, what is the distance from the rail station to his office? Assume there was a loss of time of 30 minutes while boarding the train at the station.

(A) 30 miles
(B) 60 miles
(C) 100 miles
(D) 120 miles
(E) 125 miles

Solve yourself:

5. A man swims a distance of 12 miles upstream, against the flow of the river, and the same distance downstream, with the flow of the river, to come back to his starting point. If the normal speed of the man in still water, without the effect of the flow of river, is 4 miles per hour, and the total journey took 8 hours, what is the speed of the river current in miles per hour?

Assume that, while going against the flow, the speed of the man gets reduced by an amount equal to the speed of the river. Similarly, while going with the flow, the speed of the man gets increased by an amount equal to the speed of the river.

(A) 1.5

(B) 2.0

(C) 2.5

(D) 3.0

(E) 3.5

Solve yourself:

6. Buses A and B leave City X at a gap of 30 minutes, each travelling at a speed of 40 miles per hour. Another bus, C, travels in a direction opposite to that of buses A and B and approaches them at a speed of 60 miles per hour on a parallel road. What is the time difference between when bus C crosses bus A and bus B?

(A) 12 minutes

(B) 15 minutes

(C) 20 minutes

(D) 24 minutes

(E) 30 minutes

Solve yourself:

7. If a person walked at 9 miles per hour, rather than walking at 4 miles per hour, he would have covered 7.5 miles more in the same time. What distance did the person actually cover?

(A) 1.5 miles

(B) 3.0 miles

(C) 4.5 miles

(D) 6.0 miles

(E) 13.5 miles

Solve yourself:

8. X and Y are two stations, 320 miles apart. A train, P, starts at 11:00 am from X and travels towards Y at 65 miles per hour. After traveling for four hours, it stops at a station Z, somewhere in between stations X and Y, for 30 minutes. At 2:00 pm, another train, Q, starts from Y and travels towards X at 50 miles per hour. At what time do the trains meet?

(A) 3:10 pm

(B) 3:12 pm

(C) 3:20 pm

(D) 3:30 pm

(E) 3:39 pm

Solve yourself:

9. Buses ply between two cities X and Y, traveling at the same uniform speed of 40 miles per hour. A man cycling along a straight road connecting the two cities notices that, in every 10 minutes, a bus overtakes him and in every 5 minutes, he meets a bus coming from the opposite direction. If the cyclist maintains a constant speed and all buses have a constant time interval between them, what is the speed of the cyclist, in miles per hour?

(A) 6.7

(B) 12.0

(C) 13.3

(D) 15.0

(E) 16.6

Solve yourself:

10. Traveling at a speed of 2 miles per hour above the normal speed of s miles per hour, a man can cover a distance of d miles in one hour less time. Which of the following denotes the correct relation between s and d?

(A) $d = \dfrac{(s-1)^2}{2}$

(B) $d = \dfrac{s^2 - 2}{2}$

(C) $d = \dfrac{s^2 + 2}{2}$

(D) $d = \dfrac{s^2 - 2s}{2}$

(E) $d = \dfrac{s^2 + 2s}{2}$

Solve yourself:

11. Ten equally efficient men can complete a piece of work in 10 days, whereas it takes 15 equally efficient women to complete it in 6 days. If 15 such equally efficient men and 9 such equally efficient women undertake to complete the work, how many days will they take to complete it?

(A) 3

(B) 4

(C) $6\dfrac{3}{4}$

(D) 12

(E) $18\dfrac{3}{5}$

Solve yourself:

12. 32 equally efficient men and 32 equally efficient boys can together complete a certain job in 3 days. 6 such equally efficient men and 24 such equally efficient boys can together complete the same work in 8 days. In how many days can 16 such equally efficient men and 4 such equally efficient boys complete the same work?

(A) 3

(B) 4

(C) 8

(D) 12

(E) 16

Solve yourself:

13. 8 equally efficient boys and 12 equally efficient men can complete a project of making a hundred clay toys in 9 days. If each boy takes twice the time taken by a man to complete the project, in how many days will 12 such equally efficient men complete the same project?

(A) $4\dfrac{1}{2}$

(B) $6\dfrac{3}{4}$

(C) 8

(D) 12

(E) 16

Solve yourself:

14. Ann starts on a job and does $\dfrac{7}{10}$ of the total work all by herself in 14 days. Joe joins her and they both complete the remaining work after another 2 days. How many days would it take Joe to complete the entire work all by himself?

(A) 4

(B) 8

(C) 9

(D) 10

(E) 12

Solve yourself:

15. A boat sprung a leak in the middle of a journey. The crew realized the same after some time, by then some water had already entered. It was calculated that 5 crew members would take 6 hours to remove all the water that had entered the boat. However, if a 6th crew member joined them, the task would be accomplished in 4 hours. How long would it take to remove all the water from the boat if there were 8 crew members? Assume that water keeps entering the leak at a constant rate and all crew members are equally efficient. Also, once all the water is emptied, the members would block the leak to prevent any further water from entering the boat.

(A) 2.4 hours

(B) 2.5 hours

(C) 3.2 hours

(D) 3.5 hours

(E) 3.6 hours

Solve yourself:

16. A certain number of equally efficient men can complete a job in 40 days. If there were 5 more men instead, the work could be completed in 10 days less than before. How many men were in the beginning?

(A) 12

(B) 15

(C) 18

(D) 20

(E) 24

Solve yourself:

17. John does half as much work as Pete in one-sixth of the time. If together they take 10 hours to complete a work, how many hours would Pete take to complete the work alone?

   (A) 15
   (B) 20
   (C) 30
   (D) 36
   (E) 40

   Solve yourself:

18. Amy and Bob can complete a piece of work in 45 days and 40 days, respectively. They began to work together but Amy left after few days. If Bob completed the remaining work in 23 days, after how many days did Amy leave?

   (A) 7
   (B) 8
   (C) 9
   (D) 10
   (E) 12

   Solve yourself:

19. A contractor employed 30 equally efficient men for constructing a building in 30 days. However, 10 days later, the men had completed only 25 percent of the work. How many more such equally efficient men should the contractor employ to complete the work on time?

   (A) 12
   (B) 15
   (C) 20
   (D) 25
   (E) 45

Solve yourself:

20. Amy and Bob can complete a work in 30 days and 20 days, respectively. Amy and Bob decide to work together. However, Bob left the work 3 days before it was completed. For how many days did the entire work last?

    (A) 9

    (B) 10

    (C) $10\frac{4}{5}$

    (D) 12

    (E) $13\frac{4}{5}$

Solve yourself:

21. A sum of money is invested at simple interest, partly at 4% and remaining at 7% annual rates of interest. After two years, the total interest obtained was $2100. If the total investment is $18000, what was the sum of money invested at 4% annual rate of interest?

    (A) $5500

    (B) $6000

    (C) $7000

    (D) $10500

    (E) $11000

Solve yourself:

22. A man invested two equal sums of money in two banks at simple interest, one offering annual rate of interest of 10% and the other, a rate of 20%. If the difference between the interests earned after two years is between $120 and $140, exclusive, which of the following could be the difference between the amounts earned for the same amounts of money, invested at the same rates of interest as above, but at compound interest?

(A) $130

(B) $135

(C) $138

(D) $154

(E) $162

Solve yourself:

23. A sum of money, p, invested at compound interest with $r\%$ annual rate of interest and another sum of money, q, invested at simple interest with $(2r)\%$ annual rate of interest accumulate the same interest after two years. Which of the following gives the correct relation between p and q?

(A) $q = p\left(1 + \dfrac{r}{100}\right)$

(B) $q = \dfrac{p}{r}\left(1 + \dfrac{r}{100}\right)^2$

(C) $q = \dfrac{p}{4}\left(1 + \dfrac{r}{100}\right)^2$

(D) $q = 4p\left(1 + \dfrac{r}{100}\right)$

(E) $q = \dfrac{p}{4}\left(2 + \dfrac{r}{100}\right)$

Solve yourself:

24. The difference between the interests accumulated if a sum of money is invested at 10% simple interest for two years and the same sum of money invested at 20% compound interest for two years is $87. What is the sum of money invested?

(A) $160

(B) $170

(C) $200

(D) $220

(E) $240

Solve yourself:

25. A man borrowed a certain sum of money from a friend and guaranteed to pay back the entire amount along with the interest accumulated in two equal annual payments of $200 each, starting from the next year. What is the sum of money the man had borrowed if interest is calculated at an annual 20% rate under compound interest?

(A) $400.00

(B) $397.20

(C) $359.10

(D) $332.40

(E) $305.56

Solve yourself:

26. A sum of money, p, invested at 6% annual rate of interest under simple interest fetches $120 more interest than another sum of money, one-third of the previous sum, at twice the rate of interest under simple interest in two years' more time than in the previous scenario. If $p > 2000$, and time t is an integer less than 7, what is the value of p?

(A) $2400

(B) $3000

(C) $3600

(D) $4000

(E) $4500

Solve yourself:

27. A sum of money invested at 20% annual rate of interest for 3 years amounts to the same value as the amount on the same sum of money invested at r% annual rate of compound interest for 2 years. What is the value of r? Assume $\sqrt{1.2} = 1.1$

   (A) 24%

   (B) 30%

   (C) 32%

   (D) 38%

   (E) 40%

   Solve yourself:

28. Amy invested half of her savings at simple interest and the rest at compound interest, both at the same annual rate of interest. After two years she earned interests of $180 and $189 from the simple interest account and the compound interest account, respectively. What was the value of the total investment made by Amy?

   (A) $600

   (B) $750

   (C) $900

   (D) $1200

   (E) $1800

   Solve yourself:

29. A sum of money is invested at a fixed annual rate of interest under compound interest. If the amount in the beginning of the third year is $1200, and the amount in the beginning of the fourth year is $1440, what is the amount invested, rounded to the nearest tens?

   (A) $640

   (B) $690

   (C) $800

   (D) $830

   (E) $1040

Solve yourself:

30. An investment of $2000 was made at a certain annual rate of interest under compound interest. If, after 6 years, the investment becomes $8000, what is the rate of interest? Assume that $\sqrt[3]{2} = 1.25$

  (A) 20%
  (B) 25%
  (C) 33%
  (D) 40%
  (E) 50%

Solve yourself:

31. In a group of 12 boys if two boys, aged 15 years and 18 years, are replaced by three other boys, the average age of the group drops by 1 year. If the average age, in years, of the boys originally present in the group is an integer value between 12 and 15, inclusive, and the average of the three new boys is an integer, what is the average age of the three new boys?

  (A) 9
  (B) 10
  (C) 11
  (D) 12
  (E) 13

Solve yourself:

32. What is the simple average rate of increase in population of a country per decade if the population increased by 20% in the first decade, 25% in the second decade and 15% in the third decade?

(A) 20.0%

(B) 21.7%

(C) 45.0%

(D) 56.4%

(E) 60.0%

Solve yourself:

33. Four teams, A, B, C and D, have average weights of 30 kg, 35 kg, 40 kg and 50 kg, respectively. If there are 40 students in all the teams taken together and the average weight of all the students is 40 kg, what is the maximum number of students in section C? There must be at least 2 students in each team.

(A) 30

(B) 31

(C) 32

(D) 33

(E) 34

Solve yourself:

34. The average age of a family of 7 members is 25 years. If the youngest member is 4 years old, what was the average age of the family, in years, when the youngest member was born?

(A) 18.5

(B) 21.0

(C) 23.6

(D) 24.5

(E) 27.0

Solve yourself:

35. The average price of a chair, a table, and a cot is $70; the average price of a table, a cot and a bookshelf is $85. If the price of the book-shelf is $70, what is the price of the chair?

(A) $25

(B) $30

(C) $35

(D) $40

(E) $45

Solve yourself:

36. In a group of friends, $\frac{1}{4}$ of the friends, working as managers and having an average salary of $3000, get 50% increase in their salaries. The remaining friends, working as supervisors and having an average salary of $1800, get 20% increase in their salaries. What was the average salary of the entire group after their salaries were increased?

(A) $2540

(B) $2678

(C) $2745

(D) $3240

(E) $3330

Solve yourself:

37. In a class having 50 students, two groups, A and B, are formed having students in the ratio 2 : 3 respectively. The average weight of all the students is 40 kg. The average weight of the students in group A is 5 kg less than that of the other group. If Joe shifts from group B to group A, the average weights of the sections become equal. What is Joe's weight?

(A) 37 kg

(B) 42 kg

(C) 75 kg

(D) 80 kg

(E) 100 kg

Solve yourself:

38. Eight friends raised some funds among themselves to purchase a camera. Seven of them contributed $120 each, while the other contributed $21 more than the average of all eight friends. If they raised an amount just sufficient to purchase the camera, what was the price of the camera?

(A) $645

(B) $690

(C) $778

(D) $864

(E) $984

Solve yourself:

39. In a company, the average salary of senior managers is $4500 higher than that of junior managers. If there are 80 junior managers and 100 senior managers, the average salary of all junior and senior managers together is how much higher than the average salary of the junior managers?

(A) $2000

(B) $2250

(C) $2500

(D) $2750

(E) $3000

Solve yourself:

40. A store sells laptops and mobiles. Each laptop is priced at $1200 and each mobile is priced at $900. On a particular Tuesday morning, there were 20 items in all and the average price of the items was $1080. After selling few laptops (no mobiles were sold), the average price of the remaining items became $1000 just before the store was shut for the day. If no items were added to his stock, how many laptops were sold on Tuesday?

(A)   4

(B)   8

(C)   9

(D)   10

(E)   12

Solve yourself:

41. One train left the station and traveled towards its destination at a speed of 65 miles per hour. Sometime later, another train left the same station traveling in the opposite direction of the first train, going at a speed of 105 miles per hour. After the first train had traveled for 14 hours it was 1960 miles apart from the second train. How long after the first train did the second train start?

(A)   4 hours

(B)   4 hours 20 minutes

(C)   5 hours

(D)   6 hours 10 minutes

(E)   6 hours 30 minutes

Solve yourself:

42. A man traveling from one city to another travelled the first one-third of the distance at an average speed of 50 miles per hour, the remaining at a speed of 20 miles per hour and took 4 hours and 48 minutes for the entire journey, what is the distance (in miles) between the two cities?

(A) 40

(B) 80

(C) 120

(D) 160

(E) 180

Solve yourself:

43. A train left city LA for city NY at 1:00 pm. At 5:00 pm, another train, traveling at 20 miles per hour faster than the first train, left a city which is 20 miles behind LA, along the same line joining LA and NY, and travelled towards NY. The second train caught up with the first train at 9:00 pm. How fast (in miles per hour) was the second train travelling?

(A) 15

(B) 20

(C) 25

(D) 35

(E) 40

Solve yourself:

44. A man travelled distances in the ratio of 6 : 4 : 5 at speeds in the ratio 2 : 3 : 5, respectively. If the total distance he travelled was 150 miles and the total time taken was 8 hours, what would be the time, in hours, taken by the man had he travelled the entire distance at the greatest of the three speeds?

(A) 3.5

(B) 4.0

(C) 4.5

(D) 6.0

(E) 7.5

Solve yourself:

45. During a journey, a boy travelled at x miles per hour for the first d miles. Thereafter, he increased his speed by 20% for the remaining part of the journey. He realized that the remaining distance was 50% greater than the distance he had already covered. Had the boy covered the entire distance at x miles per hour, what would be the ratio of the total time taken to cover the entire distance for the original scenario and for the revised scenario?

(A) 3 : 5

(B) 4 : 7

(C) 13 : 25

(D) 9 : 10

(E) 1 : 1

Solve yourself:

46. A man drove a car and travelled a distance of 360 miles. Had the speed of the car been less by 4 miles per hour, the time taken to travel the same distance would have been 3 hours greater than what it took initially. What was the actual speed, in miles per hour, of the car?

(A) 15

(B) 18

(C) 20

(D) 24

(E) 30

Solve yourself:

47. A man travelled x miles at an average speed of 5 miles per hour. He then went on to cover another 10 miles at an average speed of 10 miles per hour. If $1 \leq x \leq 10$, which of the following could be the percent by which his total travel time was greater than it would have been had he traveled at constant rate of 10 miles per hour?

   (A) 8%

   (B) 23%

   (C) 54%

   (D) 67%

   (E) 75%

   Solve yourself:

48. A and B are assigned to complete a project. If A worked alone, it would take him 15 hours to finish the work. However, if B worked alone, he would have required 18 hours to complete the project. If A works for the first 6 hours, and then both A and B work on the project for another 3 hours, how long, in hours, would it take for B to complete the remaining work?

   (A) $4\frac{1}{5}$

   (B) $5\frac{1}{3}$

   (C) $5\frac{3}{5}$

   (D) $6\frac{1}{2}$

   (E) $6\frac{5}{6}$

   Solve yourself:

49. Pumps A, B and C are connected to a tank. A and B, working simultaneously, can fill the tank in 12 hours. A and C, working simultaneously, can fill the tank in 15 hours; while B and C, working simultaneously, can fill the tank in 20 hours. In how many hours would A, B and C, working simultaneously, fill the tank?

   (A) 5

(B)   8

(C)   10

(D)   15

(E) $15\frac{2}{3}$

Solve yourself:

50. A and B can together complete a work in 24 days, while C alone can complete the same work in 28 days. A first works with C for 4 days, following which he leaves and B continues with C for another 10 days. Finally, B completes the remaining work in another 4 days. In how many days would B alone complete the entire work?

(A)   120

(B)   90

(C)   60

(D)   40

(E)   30

Solve yourself:

51. A and B start walking from a point P towards a point Q. The ratio of the speeds of A and B is 7 : 1. After reaching point Q, A immediately returns towards P and meets B who is still walking. If the distance from P to Q is 200 meters, what is the distance, in meters, of the meeting point from point P?

(A)   33

(B)   50

(C)   67

(D)   120

(E)   150

Solve yourself:

52. Bob starts from a point A and goes towards a point B, 150 miles away, at a speed of 60 miles per hour. At the same time, Chad starts from point B and goes towards point A at a speed of 30 miles per hour. After Chad has traveled 30 miles, he makes a stop of 15 minutes and then resumes his journey at his normal speed. At what distance, in miles, from point B do Bob and Chad meet?

   (A) 30
   (B) 45
   (C) 60
   (D) 90
   (E) 105

Solve yourself:

53. A can complete a work in x days and B can complete the same work in kx days, where k is a positive integer. If the number of days taken by A and B together to complete the work is an integer less than 5, how many possible values of the ordered set of (k, x) exist?

   (A) Three
   (B) Four
   (C) Five
   (D) Eight
   (E) Nine

Solve yourself:

54.   A and B start from points P and Q, at speeds 20 miles per hour and 15 miles per hour, respectively. A travels towards Q, while B travels towards P; and they meet at a point M on the way. Had B travelled at 18 miles per hour, A and B would have met at a point N, which is 6 miles farther from M. What is the distance, in miles, from Q to M?

(A)   25

(B)   30

(C)   57

(D)   76

(E)   133

Solve yourself:

55.   Running on a 15-mile circular loop in the same direction, A ran at a constant rate of 12 miles per hour and B ran at a constant rate of 10 miles per hour. If they began running from the same point on the loop at the same time, after how many hours did the integer number of laps completed by A is exactly one more than the integer number of laps completed by B?

(A)   4.5

(B)   5.0

(C)   6.0

(D)   7.5

(E)   15.0

Solve yourself:

56.   In a test, Jane solved 20 problem-solving questions and 10 data-sufficiency questions in the stipulated time. Jane always takes twice as much time to solve a data-sufficiency question as a problem-solving question. If she wants to complete 30 problem-solving questions and 20 data-sufficiency questions in the same stipulated time, by what percent should she reduce the time she takes to solve a question? Assume that all questions of the same category take the same amount of time.

(A)   33.3%

(B)   42.9%

(C) 50.0%

(D) 66.7%

(E) 75.0%

Solve yourself:

57. Brenda takes 45 strides per minute during morning walks (Each stride is 2 feet long). However, while going to school, her speed is 50% higher and each stride is 2.5 feet long. How many more strides does she take per minute while going to school than the number of strides per minute she takes during her morning walks?

(A) 9

(B) 18

(C) 36

(D) 45

(E) 54

Solve yourself:

58. With five identical servers working at a constant rate, an internet service provider processes 45,000 search requests per hour. How many additional servers, identical to the ones already installed, does the internet service provider need to add, such that the service provider can process at least 216,000 search requests in three hours? Assume that each search request takes the same amount of time.

(A) 1

(B) 3

(C) 4

(D) 5

(E) 8

Solve yourself:

59. Jamaica Blue Mountain coffee beans cost $19.00 a pound, and Colombian coffee beans cost $4.00 a pound. How many pounds of Jamaica Blue Mountain beans must be added to 8 pounds of Colombian beans to produce a blend that, if sold at $8.40 a pound, results in 20 percent profit?

    (A) 1.5

    (B) 2.0

    (C) 2.5

    (D) 3.0

    (E) 4.0

Solve yourself:

60. During a trip, Francine traveled x percent of the total distance at an average speed of 40 miles per hour and the rest of the distance at an average speed of 60 miles per hour. In terms of x, what was Francine's average speed for the entire trip?

    (A) $\dfrac{180 - x}{2}$

    (B) $\dfrac{x + 60}{4}$

    (C) $\dfrac{300 - x}{5}$

    (D) $\dfrac{600}{115 - x}$

    (E) $\dfrac{12000}{x + 200}$

Solve yourself:

61. The average (arithmetic mean) cost per book for the 12 books on a certain table is k dollars. If a book that costs 18 dollars is removed from the table and replaced by a book that costs 42 dollars, then in terms of k, what will be the average cost per book, in dollars, for the books on the table?

    (A) $k + 2$

    (B) $k - 2$

(C) $12 + \dfrac{24}{k}$

(D) $12 - \dfrac{24}{k}$

(E) $12k - 6$

Solve yourself:

62.   The average (arithmetic mean) score on a test taken by 10 students was x. If the average score for 5 of the students was 8, what was the average score, in terms of x, for the remaining 5 students who took the test?

(A) $2x - 8$

(B) $x - 4$

(C) $8 - 2x$

(D) $16 - x$

(E) $8 - \dfrac{x}{2}$

Solve yourself:

63.   Leo can buy a certain computer for p dollars in State A, where the sales tax is t percent, or he can buy the same computer for P dollars in State B, where the sales tax is T percent. Is the total cost of the computer greater in State A than in State B?

(1) $t > T$

(2) $pt > PT$

Solve yourself:

64.   For telephone calls between two particular cities, a telephone company charges $0.40 per minute if the calls are placed between 5:00 am and 9:00 pm and $0.25 per minute if the

calls are placed between 9:00 pm and 5:00 am. If the charge for a call between the two cities placed at 8:00 pm was $30.00, how much would a call of the same duration have cost if it had been placed at 11:00 pm?

(A) $5.00

(B) $6.25

(C) $12.50

(D) $16.00

(E) $21.00

Solve yourself:

65. The manager of a theater noted that for every 16 admission tickets sold, the theater sells 3 bags of popcorn at $5.25 each, 4 sodas at $4.50 each, and 2 candy bars at $3.00 each. What is the approximate average (arithmetic mean) amount of all these snack sales per ticket sold?

(A) $2.00

(B) $2.10

(C) $2.50

(D) $3.50

(E) $4.40

Solve yourself:

66. A man travels 720 miles in 8 hours, partly by air and partly by train. If he had travelled all the way by air, he would have saved $\frac{4}{5}$ of the time he was in train and would have arrived at his destination 4 hours early. What is the distance, in miles, travelled by the man by air?

(A) 480

(B) 520

(C) 540

(D) 600

(E) 660

Solve yourself:

67. A man covered $\frac{1}{3}$ of the distance to his destination at 20 miles per hour, $\frac{1}{2}$ of the remaining distance at 12 miles per hour and remaining distance at 40 miles per hour. What was his average speed, in miles per hour, for the whole journey?

(A) 12.1

(B) 16.0

(C) 18.9

(D) 22.5

(E) 30.7

Solve yourself:

68. Jane lives x floors above the ground floor of a high-rise building. It takes her 30 seconds per floor to walk down the steps and 2 seconds per floor to ride the elevator. If it takes Jane the same amount of time to walk down the steps to the ground floor as to wait for the elevator for 7 minutes and ride down, then what is the value of x?

(A) 4

(B) 7

(C) 14

(D) 15

(E) 16

Solve yourself:

69. Mary passed a certain gas station on a highway while traveling west at a constant speed of 50 miles per hour. Then, 15 minutes later, Paul passed the same gas station while traveling west at a constant speed of 60 miles per hour. If both drivers maintained their speeds and both remained on the highway for at least 2 hours, how long, in minutes, after he passed the gas station did Paul catch up with Mary?

(A) 30

(B) 45

(C) 60

(D) 75

(E) 85

Solve yourself:

70. A man, while traveling in a car from City X to City Y, to pick up his son, overtakes a bus traveling in the same direction, at 10:00 am. On reaching City Y at 2:00 pm, the man picks up his son and turns back towards City X, without any loss of time. If, on the way back, the man meets the same bus which he had overtaken earlier, at 3:00 pm, when would the bus reach City Y? Assume that the man and the bus travel throughout with uniform speeds.

(A) 3:40 pm

(B) 3:50 pm

(C) 4:20 pm

(D) 4:30 pm

(E) 4:40 pm

Solve yourself:

71. Two hours after Jack started walking from P to Q, a distance of 25 miles; Bob started walking along the same road in the same direction as Jack. If Jack's walking rate was 3 miles per hour and Bob's was 5 miles per hour, how many miles before Q did Bob overtake Jack?

(A) 9

(B) 10

(C) 12

(D) 15

(E) 16

Solve yourself:

72. Pumping alone at their respective constant rates, one inlet pipe fills an empty tank to $\frac{1}{2}$ of capacity in 3 hours and a second inlet pipe fills the same empty tank to $\frac{2}{3}$ of capacity in 6 hours. How many hours will it take both pipes, pumping simultaneously at their respective constant rates, to fill the empty tank to capacity?

    (A) 3.25

    (B) 3.60

    (C) 4.20

    (D) 4.40

    (E) 5.52

Solve yourself:

73. Running at their respective constant rates, machine X takes 2 days longer to produce w widgets than machine Y. At these rates, if the two machines together produce $\frac{5}{4}w$ widgets in 3 days, how many days would it take machine X alone to produce $2w$ widgets?

    (A) 4

    (B) 6

    (C) 8

    (D) 10

    (E) 12

Solve yourself:

74. A water sample has 10 percent of impurities present. If after each purification process, the impurity level reduces by 60 percent of the present value, what is the minimum number of times that the water sample needs to be purified in order to reduce the impurities present to at most 1 percent?

    (A) 2

    (B) 3

    (C) 4

    (D) 5

    (E) 6

    Solve yourself:

75. On a certain day, Tim invested $1,000 at 10 percent annual interest, compounded annually, and Lana invested $2,000 at 5 percent annual interest, compounded annually. The total amount of interest earned by Tim's investment in the first 2 years was how much greater than the total amount of interest earned by Lana's investment in the first 2 years?

    (A) $5

    (B) $15

    (C) $50

    (D) $100

    (E) $105

    Solve yourself:

76. For telephone calls between two particular cities, a telephone company charges $0.40 per minute if the calls are placed between 5:00 am and 9:00 pm and $0.25 per minute if the calls are placed between 9:00 pm and 5:00 am. If the charge for a call between the two cities placed at 1:00 pm was $10.00, how much would a call of the same duration have cost if it had been placed at 11:00 pm?

    (A) $3.75

    (B) $6.25

    (C) $9.85

(D) $10.00

(E) $16.00

Solve yourself:

3.2 Data Sufficiency

Data sufficiency questions have five standard options. They are listed below and will not be repeated for each question.

(A) Statement (1) ALONE is sufficient, but statement (2) ALONE is not sufficient to answer the question asked.

(B) Statement (2) ALONE is sufficient, but statement (1) ALONE is not sufficient to answer the question asked.

(C) both the statements (1) and (2) TOGETHER are sufficient to answer the question asked, but NEITHER statement ALONE is sufficient to answer the question asked.

(D) EACH statement ALONE is sufficient to answer the question asked.

(E) Statements (1) and (2) TOGETHER are NOT sufficient to answer the question asked, and additional data specific to the problem are needed.

77. If a, b, c and d are positive numbers such that $a < b < c < d$, can b be the average of the four numbers a, b, c and d?

    (1)   The average of c and d is $\dfrac{3b}{2}$

    (2)   The average of a, b and c is b

Solve yourself:

78. If a group of new students join a class, the average age of the class decreases by 1 year. What was the average age of the original students of the class?

    (1)   The average age of the students in the new group is 15 years.

    (2)   When the new group of students joins the class, the strength of the class increases by a number equal to the initial average age of the students in the class.

Solve yourself:

79. If n is an integer, is the average of the first n positive integers an integer?

    (1)   The average of the first $2n$ positive integers is not an integer.

    (2)   The average of the first $\dfrac{n}{2}$ positive integers is an integer.

Solve yourself:

80. If m and n are positive integers such that $m > n$, is the average of the first $(m + n)$ integers greater than thrice the average of of the first $(m - n)$ integers?

    (1) $m > 2n$

    (2) $m < 3n$

Solve yourself:

81. Are the number of people initially in the group at least 8?

    (1)   The average age of the group is less than 22 years.

    (2)   If 3 people with average age 44 years leave the group, the average age of the group decreases to half the value.

    Solve yourself:

82. Two varieties of rice, a kg of one, priced at $\$x$ per kg and b kg of the other, priced at $\$(3x)$ per kg, are mixed together. Is the average price of the mixture greater than $\$\left(\dfrac{3}{2}x\right)$?

    (1) $a > 2b$

    (2) $a = 3b$

    Solve yourself:

83. Is the average of numbers with base 2 and exponents consecutive integers an integer?

    (1)   The least power (exponents) of 2 is 7.

    (2)   The number of powers of 2 is 4.

    Solve yourself:

84. The average daily salary of the entire staff of a factory consisting only of engineers and supervisors is $50. If each engineer and each supervisor gets the same salary respectively, is the number of engineers in the factory greater than half the total staff?

(1)   The average daily salary of 40% of the engineers and 60% of the supervisors is $45

(2)   The average daily salary of 60% of the engineers and 40% of the supervisors is $55

Solve yourself:

85. What was the temperature on Monday?

(1)   The average temperature on Monday, Tuesday, Wednesday and Thursday was 30° C.

(2)   The average for Tuesday, Wednesday, Thursday and Friday was 25° C.

Solve yourself:

86. If each test is scored out of 90, what was Dan's average mark in the first four tests?

(1)   Dan received 88 marks in the fifth test.

(2)   The difference between Dan's average mark after the first four tests and the average mark after the first five tests is an integer.

Solve yourself:

87. A and B start from their homes at a previously agreed time and travel towards each other at their respective uniform speed. On the way, they meet at a point X. If A had been late in starting from his home by t minutes, they would have met at another point Y. What is the value of t?

(1)   A and B travel at speeds of 6 km per hour and 12 km per hour, respectively.

(2)   The distance between the points X and Y is 1.2 km.

Solve yourself:

88. A man covers a certain distance upstream (sailing against the current) in a boat in 6 hours. How long would he take to travel the same distance upstream in the river if he uses a boat that is twice as fast in still water as the earlier one?

    (1)   The man takes 4 hours to cover the same distance downstream (sailing with the current) using the slower boat.

    (2)   The distance the man covers upstream is 12 miles.

Solve yourself:

89. If a man covers one part of his journey at a particular speed and the remaining part of the journey at another speed, can the average speed of the man be greater than 23 miles per hour?

    (1)   The distances the man covered at different speeds are in the ratio 4 : 5.

    (2)   The two different speeds with which the man travelled are 16 miles per hour and 30 miles per hour.

Solve yourself:

90. A and B start from two points at the same time, P and Q, respectively, and travel towards each other. What is the ratio of the speeds of A and B?

    (1)   They meet at a point 300 meters from the end Q.

    (2)   Had A moved towards Q and B moved in the same direction as A, A would have caught up with B at a point 400 meters from Q.

Solve yourself:

91. A man travels a distance of x miles at a speed of p miles per hour and another distance of y miles at a speed of q miles per hour ($p \neq q$). Is the average speed of the man $\left(\dfrac{p+q}{2}\right)$ miles per hour?

(1) $x = y$

(2) $2py = qx$

Solve yourself:

92. A boy usually cycles to school from his home and reaches school at the scheduled time. One day, if he walked half the distance and hailed a cab for the remaining half of the distance, would he have reached school without being late?

(1)   The boy cycles at a speed which is thrice his walking speed.

(2)   The speed of the cab is thrice his cycling speed.

Solve yourself:

93. A, B and C cover a number of laps in a circular track of length 1200 meters, having started from the same point. What is the ratio of speeds of A and C?

(1)   If A and B run in the same direction, A covers 5 laps in the same time when B covers 4 laps.

(2)   If B and C run in opposite directions, B covers 400 meters when he meets C coming from the opposite direction.

Solve yourself:

94. While covering a particular distance, a boy calculated that he would reach on time if he covered the first half of the distance at 20 miles per hour and the remaining half of the distance at a higher speed. What is the total distance the boy travelled?

  (1) The boy travelled the remaining half of the distance at 40 miles per hour and reached his destination just on time.

  (2) If the boy had travelled the remaining half of the distance at 30 miles per hour, he would have reached his destination 15 minutes late.

Solve yourself:

95. A and B start from two points P and Q, respectively at the same time, and walk towards one another. They meet at a point 300 meters from Q. After meeting, both A and B walk towards point P. How far behind was B when A reached point P?

  (1) The ratio of speeds of A and B is 5 : 3

  (2) The total distance between the points P and Q is 800 meters.

Solve yourself:

96. John's speed while running is what percent greater than his speed while walking?

  (1) John takes 40 minutes to walk from his home to school and return home running.

  (2) John takes 30 minutes to run from his home to school and return home running.

Solve yourself:

97. Three friends, A, B and C are assigned to complete a work. A and B together can complete the work in 20 days, while B and C together can complete the work in 25 days. How long would C take to complete the entire work alone?

   (1) To complete the work, A works for the first 4 days alone, then B works the next 9 days alone and finally C works for 23 days alone.

   (2) B can complete the entire work in 150 days.

   Solve yourself:

98. A, B and C start working together on a project with C leaving after $\frac{1}{4}$ of the project was completed and B leaving after another $\frac{1}{4}$ of the project was completed.? Is the total duration of the project less than 16 days?

   (1) A and B can complete the project alone in 20 and 30 days, respectively.

   (2) C can complete the project alone in 25 days.

   Solve yourself:

99. If C takes twice as long to complete a work as A and B together take, how long does A, B and C together take to complete the work?

   (1) A takes twice as long to complete a work as C.

   (2) B takes 20 days to complete the same work alone.

   Solve yourself:

100. In a factory, three machines P, Q and R, manufacture items A, B and C, respectively. To prepare the final product, three units of A, two units of B and one unit of C are required. How many pieces of the final product are produced in a nine-hour working shift?

    (1)   Machine P manufactures 5 units of item A in every three hours.

    (2)   Compared to machine P, machines Q and R manufacture their respective single item 20% faster and 20% slower, respectively.

Solve yourself:

101. Two pipes, A and B, connected to a tank fill it at uniform rates of 12 liters per minute and 15 liters per minute, respectively. How long would it take to fill the tank if both the above pipes and a third filling pipe, C, are connected to the tank?

    (1)   The time taken by the pipes A and C to fill another tank, twice as large as the given tank, is 30 minutes.

    (2)   The pipe C takes 45 minutes to fill the given tank with no other pipes connected.

Solve yourself:

102. If A and B together can complete a work in 40 days, does A have the greatest efficiency among A, B and C?

    (1)   B and C together can complete the same work in 30 days.

    (2)   C can complete the same work in 50 days.

Solve yourself:

103. If the time taken to paint a wall directly varies with the area of the wall, how long would 4 men and 6 women take to paint a wall having dimensions 60 feet by 80 feet? Assume all men and women work at their uniform rates.

(1) It takes 15 men 8 hours to paint a wall having dimensions 150 feet by 90 feet.

(2) An area of 20 square feet can be painted by 2 men in 1 hour or by 1 woman in 2 hours.

Solve yourself:

104. The sum of the times taken by A, working alone, and B, also working alone, to complete a piece of work is t hours. Is $t > 20$?

   (1) The individual times taken by A and B, to complete the piece of work are positive integers.

   (2) Working together, A and B take 3 hours to complete the same work.

Solve yourself:

105. Twenty equally efficient workers were employed who can complete a piece of work in 15 days. After x days ($x \neq 0$), another n similar workers were also employed. Can the work be now completed in less than 10 days?

   (1) $n = 10$

   (2) $x = 5$

Solve yourself:

106. What is the length of each step that John takes while running?

   (1) The number of steps he takes per minute is 25 times his speed measured in meters per second.

   (2) John runs at a speed of 5 meters per second.

Solve yourself:

107. Two varieties of tea are mixed. Per pound price of the costlier variety is $15 more than per pound price of the cheaper variety. In what ratio were the two varieties of tea mixed?

    (1)   The average price of the mixture is $20 per pound.

    (2)   The average price of the mixture is $7 per pound cheaper than the costlier variety.

Solve yourself:

108. A man covers a part of his journey at 20 miles per hour and the remaining at 30 miles per hour. What is the total distance covered by the man?

    (1)   The average speed of the man is 24 miles per hour.

    (2)   The ratio of the time for which he travelled at 20 miles per hour and that for which he travelled at 30 miles per hour is 3 : 2.

Solve yourself:

109. A travels from point P to point Q, while B travels from point Q to point P. At what time do they meet on the way?

    (1)   A starts his journey at 9:00 am while B starts his journey from 11:00 am.

    (2)   A takes 9 hours to reach point Q while B takes 6 hours to reach point P.

Solve yourself:

110. A and B participate in a walkathon. If they start at the same time, will A win the contest?

    (1)   For every 5 steps taken by A, B takes 8 steps.

    (2)   3 steps of A are of the same length of 5 steps of B.

Solve yourself:

111. A boy toed and froed between points P and Q a certain number of times. What is his average speed?

    (1)   The boy covers the distance from P to Q, first leg, at a speed of 2 meters per second and returns at a speed of 4 meters per second, second leg, and keeps on toing and froing with double the speed of the previous leg.

    (2)   Once the boy attains his maximum speed, he does not go for the next leg. The maximum speed the boy can run is 16 meters per second.

Solve yourself:

112. A man covers a part of his journey by train and the rest by bus. What is the ratio of the distances he travelled by train and by bus?

    (1)   The speeds of the train and bus are 80 miles per hour and 60 miles per hour respectively.

    (2)   Had the man covered the entire journey by train at 80 miles per hour, he would have taken only $\frac{4}{5}$ of the time he actually took.

Solve yourself:

113. A boy usually walks to school from his home at a uniform speed and reaches school on time. How early will he reach school if he cycles to school from his home?

    (1)   The boy's cycling speed is thrice his walking speed.

(2) Had the boy travelled in a car at a speed twice that of his cycling speed, he would
      have reached school 10 minutes before the time he reaches while cycling.

Solve yourself:

114. A and B start from their homes at a previously agreed time and travel towards each
      other at their respective uniform speeds. On the way, they meet at a point P. If B had
      travelled at 20% higher speed, they would have met at another point Q. What is the
      distance between the homes of A and B?

      (1) A and B travel at speeds of 9 miles per hour and 15 miles per hour, respectively.

      (2) The distance between the points P and Q is 2 miles.

Solve yourself:

115. How long does a man take to cover a certain distance traveling at his normal speed?

      (1) If the man had travelled the same distance at 6 miles per hour greater than his
           normal speed, he would have taken 1 hour less than the time he would have taken
           while traveling at his normal speed.

      (2) If the man had travelled the same distance at 4 miles per hour lower than his normal
           speed, he would have taken 1 hour more than the time he would have taken while
           traveling at his normal speed.

Solve yourself:

116. A and B travel from points P and Q, respectively, towards point R, where P, Q and R lie
      along the same straight route. If point P lies 100 meters behind point Q, does A reach
      point R before B?

      (1) The distance between the points Q and R is 500 meters.

(2) If A had started from Q and B had started from P, B would have been 100 meters behind A when A would have reached R.

Solve yourself:

117. What is the average speed of the spaceship over the first 5 seconds?

    (1) The distance, in miles, travelled by the spaceship in the kth second is given by $(30k^2 - 5)$, where k is a positive integer.

    (2) The total distance, in miles, travelled by the spaceship in k seconds is given by $5k^2(2k + 3)$, where k is a positive integer.

Solve yourself:

118. A is a set of n consecutive even integers starting from a and B is a set of n consecutive even integers starting from $(a + 2n)$. What is the value of n?

    (1) The difference between the average of the integers in set A and the average of the integers in set B is 40.

    (2) The sum of the average of the integers in set A and the average of the integers in set B is 120.

Solve yourself:

119. Two pipes, A and B, can fill a tank with water in 12 hours and 8 hours, respectively. There is a third pipe, C, which is used to empty the tank. Only pipes A and B were opened initially and after x hours, pipe C was also opened. How long does it take for pipe C to empty the full tank?

    (1) Three hours after pipes A and B were opened, the tank was only half filled.

    (2) x is an integer.

Solve yourself:

120. If a group of students join a class, the average age of all the students in the class comes down by one year from the average age of the initial students, what was the initial average age of the class?

   (1) The average age of the students who join the class is 17 years.

   (2) When the new students join the class, the strength of the class increases by 50 percent.

Solve yourself:

121. Did Bob get an average of at most 79 marks in his last two tests?

   (1) Bob's average marks before taking the last two tests was 85.

   (2) Bob's average marks after taking the last two tests was 81.

Solve yourself:

122. Is the average of a group of people at least 20 yrs?

   (1) If 4 people with average age 40 years join the group, the average of the group increases by 2 years.

   (2) If 4 people with average age 40 years join the group, the average age of the group doubles in value.

Solve yourself:

123. Martin has worked for the last 30 years. If his average (arithmetic mean) annual earnings for the first 5 years was $15,000, what was his average annual earnings for the last 5 years?

(1) Martin's average annual earnings for the first 25 years was $27,000.

(2) Martin's average annual earnings for the last 25 years was $34,000.

Solve yourself:

124. On a given day, 50 people took a test designed to measure a candidate's aptitude. Some of the 50 people took the test in the morning, and the remaining took the test in the afternoon. What was the average (arithmetic mean) score on the test for the 50 examinees?

(1) The average score for the examinees who took the test in the morning was 68.

(2) The average score for the examinees who took the test in the afternoon was 74.

Solve yourself:

125. The average (arithmetic mean) of a list of numbers is what percent of the sum of the numbers?

(1) There are 8 numbers in the list.

(2) The sum of the numbers in the list is 100.

Solve yourself:

126.

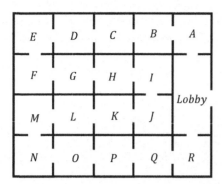

The figure above represents the floor plan of an art gallery that has a lobby and 18 rooms of equal dimensions. The doors in each room are shown by an open space on the sides, for example, room E has one door connecting to room D and another door connecting to room F. If Lisa goes from the lobby into room A at the same time that Paul goes from the lobby into room R, and each goes through all of the rooms in succession, entering by one door and exiting by the other, which room will they be in at the same time?

(1) Lisa spends $2x$ minutes in each room and Paul spends $3x$ minutes in each room.

(2) Lisa spends 10 minutes less time in each room than Paul does.

Solve yourself:

127. The total cost of an office dinner was shared equally by k of the n employees who attended the dinner. What was the total cost of the dinner?

(1) Each of the k employees who shared the cost of the dinner paid \$19.

(2) If the total cost of the dinner had been shared equally by $(k + 1)$ of the n employees who attended the dinner, each of the $(k + 1)$ employees would have paid \$18.

Solve yourself:

128. A theater has 35 rows with 27 seats in each row. How many of the seats were occupied during a certain show?

(1) During the show, there was an average (arithmetic mean) of 10 unoccupied seats per row for the front 20 rows.

(2) During the show, there was an average (arithmetic mean) of 20 unoccupied seats per row for the back 16 rows.

Solve yourself:

129. Two cars, S and T, each traveled a distance of 90 miles. Did car S use more gasoline per hour than car T?

(1) Cars S and T traveled the entire distance at the rates of 50 miles per hour and 45 miles per hour, respectively.

(2) For the entire distance, car S traveled 20 miles per gallon of gasoline and car T traveled 30 miles per gallon of gasoline.

Solve yourself:

130. Was the average (arithmetic mean) weight of the package mailed at a certain post office yesterday greater than 600 grams?

(1) The total weight of the packages mailed at the post office yesterday was greater than 14,500 grams.

(2) Fewer than 25 packages were mailed at the post office yesterday.

Solve yourself:

131. What is the value of $(n - w) + (n - x) + (n - y) + (n - z)$?

(1) The average (arithmetic mean) of w, x, y and z is n.

(2) w, x, y and z are consecutive integers.

Solve yourself:

132. What was the percent increase in the average (arithmetic mean) contribution per member of a certain public radio station from 1985 to 1995?

  (1) Total contributions by members increased from $505,210 in 1985 to $1,225,890 in 1995.

  (2) The number of members exactly doubled from 1985 to 1995.

Solve yourself:

133. When a group of students left a class, the average age of the class came down by 2 years. What was the final average age of the remaining students in the class?

  (1) The average age of the group of students who left the class was 22 years.

  (2) When the group of students left the class, the strength of the class went down by 40 percent.

Solve yourself:

134. In a marathon race of 1000 meters between two competitors, A and B, A ran with a speed of 10 meters per second. What was the speed of B?

  (1) A defeated B by a distance of 250 meters.

  (2) Had A allowed B to start the race from a point 100 meters ahead of him, A would have still managed to beat B by 20 seconds.

Solve yourself:

135. In a marathon, Brad ran some distance uphill at a speed of 6 miles per hour. While traveling downhill along a different route, Brad ran at a speed of 10 miles per hour. What was the distance that Brad covered uphill?

(1) The total trip (going uphill and coming downhill) took 5 hours.

(2) The average speed for the entire trip (going uphill and coming downhill) was 8 miles per hour.

Solve yourself:

© 1999-2016 Manhattan Review

Chapter 4

Answer-key

4.1   Problem Solving

(1) C	(21) C	(41) A
(2) B	(22) D	(42) C
(3) B	(23) E	(43) D
(4) D	(24) E	(44) C
(5) B	(25) E	(45) D
(6) A	(26) B	(46) D
(7) D	(27) C	(47) B
(8) B	(28) E	(48) A
(9) C	(29) D	(49) C
(10) E	(30) B	(50) E
(11) B	(31) C	(51) B
(12) C	(32) B	(52) B
(13) D	(33) D	(53) D
(14) D	(34) D	(54) C
(15) A	(35) A	(55) B
(16) B	(36) D	(56) B
(17) E	(37) E	(57) A
(18) C	(38) E	(58) B
(19) B	(39) C	(59) B
(20) E	(40) B	(60) E

(61) A	(67) C	(73) E
(62) A	(68) D	(74) B
(63) E	(69) D	(75) A
(64) E	(70) E	
(65) C	(71) B	
(66) C	(72) B	(76) B

4.2 Data Sufficiency

(77) D	(97) D	(117) D
(78) E	(98) A	(118) A
(79) B	(99) C	(119) E
(80) A	(100) C	(120) C
(81) C	(101) C	(121) C
(82) B	(102) A	(122) B
(83) C	(103) B	(123) C
(84) C	(104) C	(124) E
(85) E	(105) A	(125) A
(86) E	(106) A	(126) A
(87) C	(107) B	(127) C
(88) A	(108) E	(128) E
(89) C	(109) C	(129) C
(90) C	(110) C	(130) C
(91) D	(111) C	(131) A
(92) C	(112) C	(132) C
(93) C	(113) C	(133) C
(94) C	(114) C	(134) D
(95) D	(115) C	(135) C
(96) C	(116) C	

© 1999–2016 Manhattan Review

Chapter 5

Solutions

5.1   Problem Solving

1.   Distance travelled by Ann is between $2 \times 2 = 4$ miles and $2 \times 3 = 6$ miles.

Time taken by Ann is between 1 hour 30 minutes and 1 hour 45 minutes, i.e. $1\frac{1}{2}$ hours and $1\frac{3}{4}$ hours.

Thus, we have:

$$\text{Maximum speed of Ann} = \frac{\text{Maximum distance}}{\text{Minimum time}} = \frac{6}{1\frac{1}{2}} = 4 \text{ miles per hour}$$

$$\text{Minimum speed of Ann} = \frac{\text{Minimum distance}}{\text{Maximum time}} = \frac{4}{1\frac{3}{4}} = \frac{16}{7} = 2.28 \text{ miles per hour}$$

Since Bob travelled 3 miles farther than Ann did, total distance covered by Bob is $2 \times 3 = 6$ miles greater than that covered by Ann.

Thus, distance travelled by Bob is between 10 miles and 12 miles.

Time taken by Bob = 4 hours.

Thus, we have:

$$\text{Minimum speed of Bob} = \frac{\text{Minimum Distance}}{\text{Time}} = \frac{10}{4} = 2.5 \text{ miles per hour}$$

$$\text{Maximum speed of Bob} = \frac{\text{Maximum Distance}}{\text{Time}} = \frac{12}{4} = 3 \text{ miles per hour}$$

Working with the statements:

- Statement I:

  Thus, there is an overlap in the range of speeds of Ann and Bob.

  Thus, we may have Ann (4 miles per hour) faster than Bob (3 miles per hour) OR Bob (3 miles per hour) faster than Ann (2.28 miles per hour)

  Thus, Statement I is not true.

- Statement II:

  Ann's minimum speed is 2.28 miles per hour, while her maximum speed is 4 miles per hour.

  Thus, Ann's speed does not lie between 2 and 3 miles per hour.

  Thus, Statement II is not true.

- • Statement III:

    Maximum speed of Ann is 4 miles per hour, which is greater than the maximum

    speed of Bob, which is 3 miles per hour.

    Thus, Statement III is true.

The correct answer is option C.

2. Initial distance between the man and the bus = 500 feet.

    Distance covered by the man in the 10 seconds the bus was stationary

    = 30 × 10 = 300 feet.

    Distance remaining between the man and the bus = 500 – 300 = 200 feet.

    For the next 20 seconds, the bus was also moving at 25 feet per second.

    Thus, the relative speed between the man and the bus

    = 30 – 25 = 5 feet per second

    Since the man is still faster than the bus, the man will gain on the bus.

    Distance the man gained on the bus

    = 5 × 20 = 100 feet.

    Thus, distance remaining between the man and the bus = 200 – 100 = 100 feet.

    Since, after this, the bus speeds away at a very high speed, the distance between the man

    and the bus would increase.

    Thus, the shortest distance between the man and the bus = 100 feet.

    The correct answer is option B.

3. Let Danny travel at 60 miles per hour for x hours and at 120 miles per hour for y hours.

    Total distance travelled by Danny = $(60x + 120y)$ miles

    Total time taken by Danny = $(x + y)$ hours

    Since his average speed is 100 miles per hour, we have:

$$\frac{60x + 120y}{x + y} = 100$$

$$\Rightarrow 60x + 120y = 100x + 100y$$

$$\Rightarrow \frac{x}{y} = \frac{1}{2}$$

Thus, fraction of the time for which Danny travelled at 60 miles per hour $= \frac{1}{1 + 2} = \frac{1}{3}$

The correct answer is option B.

Alternate approach:

You can deal with this question using a single variable.

Let Danny travel at 60 miles per hour for 1 hours and at 120 miles per hour for p hours.

Total distance travelled by Danny $= (60 + 120p)$ miles

Total time taken by Danny $= (1 + p)$ hours

Since his average speed is 100 miles per hour, we have:

$$\frac{60 + 120p}{1 + p} = 100$$

$$\Rightarrow 60 + 120p = 100 + 100p$$

$$\Rightarrow 20p = 40 \Rightarrow p = 2$$

Thus, fraction of the time for which Danny travelled at 60 miles per hour $= \frac{1}{1 + p} = \frac{1}{1 + 2} = \frac{1}{3}$

4. Let the man travelled distance d miles by car and the remaining $(150 - d)$ miles by train.

Time taken by car $= \dfrac{d}{30}$ hours.

Time taken by train $= \dfrac{150 - d}{60}$ hours.

Time taken while boarding $= \dfrac{1}{2}$ hours.

Thus, total time $= \left(\dfrac{d}{30} + \dfrac{150 - d}{60} + \dfrac{1}{2}\right)$ hours $= \left(\dfrac{180 + d}{60}\right)$ hours.

Thus, we have:

$$\frac{180 + d}{60} = 3.5$$

$$\Rightarrow d = 30$$

Thus, the required distance = 150 – 30 = 120 miles.

The correct answer is option D.

5. Let the speed of the current be r miles per hour.

Thus, speed of the man while going upstream = $(4 - r)$ miles per hour

Speed of the man while going downstream = $(4 + r)$ miles per hour

Thus, time taken to cover 12 miles upstream = $\left(\dfrac{12}{4 - r}\right)$ hours

Time taken to cover 12 miles downstream = $\left(\dfrac{12}{4 + r}\right)$ hours

Since the total time for the trip was 8 hours, we have:

$$\dfrac{12}{4 - r} + \dfrac{12}{4 + r} = 8$$

Solving the above equation is difficult, so it is best to use the options to determine the value of r.

We observe that, for $r = 2$, we have $4 - r = 2 \Rightarrow \dfrac{12}{4 - r} = 6$, and also,

$4 + r = 6 \Rightarrow \dfrac{12}{4 + r} = 2$.

Thus, $6 + 2 = 8$ – Satisfies

The correct answer is option B.

6. Since the buses A and B leave at a gap of 30 minutes, i.e. $\dfrac{1}{2}$ an hour and they travel at 40 miles per hour, the distance between the buses

$= 40 \times \dfrac{1}{2} = 20$ miles

Let bus C meets one of the other two buses at some time.

The second bus is 20 miles away from bus C.

Since both the other bus and bus C travel in opposite directions, their relative speed

$= 40 + 60 = 100$ miles per hour

Thus, time taken by bus C to meet the other bus

$= \dfrac{20}{100} = \dfrac{1}{5}$ hour

$$= \frac{1}{5} \times 60 = 12 \text{ minutes}$$

Thus, the time difference is 12 minutes.

The correct answer is option A.

7. Let the distance covered by that person be d miles.

Time taken while walking at 4 miles per hour = $\left(\dfrac{d}{4}\right)$ hours

Distance he covers while walking at 9 miles per hour = $(d + 7.5)$ miles

Thus, time taken = $\left(\dfrac{d + 7.5}{9}\right)$ hours

Since the time is same in both the cases, we have:

$$\frac{d}{4} = \frac{d + 7.5}{9}$$

$$=> 9d = 4d + 30$$

$$=> d = 6$$

The correct answer is option D.

Alternate approach:

Difference in speeds = 9 – 4 = 5 miles per hour

Difference in distance = 7.5 miles

The difference in distance is due to his higher speed.

Thus, the time for which he travelled = $\dfrac{7.5}{5}$ = 1.5 hours

Thus, actual distance covered = 1.5 × 4 = 6 miles.

8. Distance travelled by train P in 4 hours, i.e. by 3:00 pm = 4 × 65 = 260 miles

Distance travelled by train Q in 1 hour, i.e. by 3:00 pm = 50 miles

Since the distance between the stations is 320 miles, the distance between the trains at 3:00 pm

= 320 – (260 + 50) = 10 miles

We know that train P is stationary for the next 30 minutes.

Distance covered by train Q in 30 minutes, i.e. $\frac{1}{2}$ an hour = $50 \times \frac{1}{2}$ = 25 miles.

Since 25 miles is greater than the distance between the trains (10 miles), the trains would meet at a time when train P was still stationary.

Thus, time taken by train Q to meet train P

$= \frac{10}{50}$ hour $= \frac{1}{5}$ hour

$= \frac{1}{5} \times 60$ minutes = 12 minutes

Thus, time of meeting is 3:12 pm

The correct answer is option B.

9. Let the speed of the man be x miles per hour.

   Speed of each bus = 40 miles per hour.

   Let the time interval between any two buses be t hours.

   (This means that, a person, standing at any point on the road, will observe buses coming from either direction at a constant time difference, i.e. if he sees one bus at 12:00 going from X to Y, he will observe the next bus, going from Y to X, t hours after 12, the next bus going from X to Y, $2t$ hours after 12, and so on.)

   Let us consider the buses moving in the same direction as the cyclist:

   Since the time interval between the two buses is t hours, the distance between the two buses = $40t$ miles

   The relative speed of the cyclist and the second bus, both moving in the same direction

   $= (40 - x)$ miles per hour

   Thus, time taken by the second bus to overtake the cyclist

   $= \left(\frac{40t}{40 - x} \right)$ hours

   Thus, we have:

   $\frac{40t}{40 - x} = 10$

   $=> 40t = 10 \, (40 - x) \ldots (i)$

Let us consider the buses moving in the opposite direction to the cyclist:

Since the time interval between the two buses is t hours, the distance between the two buses is also $40t$ miles

The relative speed of the cyclist and the second bus, both moving in the same direction

$= (40 + x)$ miles per hour

Thus, time taken by the second bus to overtake the cyclist

$= \left(\dfrac{40t}{40 + x} \right)$ hours

Thus, we have:

$\dfrac{40t}{40 + x} = 5$

$=> 40t = 5 (40 + x) \dots (ii)$

Thus, from (i) and (ii), we have:

$10 (40 - x) = 5 (40 + x)$

$=> 80 - 2x = 40 + x$

$=> x = \dfrac{40}{3} = 13.3$

The correct answer is option C.

10. Traveling at normal speed s, time taken to cover distance d

$= \dfrac{d}{s}$ hours

New speed $= (s + 2)$ miles per hour

Thus, time taken

$= \dfrac{d}{s + 2}$ hours

Since the time difference is 1 hour, we have:

$\dfrac{d}{s} - \dfrac{d}{s + 2} = 1$

$=> \dfrac{d (s + 2 - s)}{s (s + 2)} = 1$

$=> 2d = s^2 + 2s$

$=> d = \dfrac{s^2 + 2s}{2}$

The correct answer is option E.

11. 10 men can complete a work in 10 days.

Thus, to complete the work in 1 day, number of men required = $10 \times 10 = 100$

15 women can complete a work in 6 days.

Thus, to complete the work in 1 day, number of women required = $15 \times 6 = 90$

Thus, we have:

100 men $\equiv$ 90 women

$\Rightarrow$ 15 men $\equiv \dfrac{90}{100} \times 15 = 13.5$ women

Thus, 15 men and 9 women together $\equiv (13.5 + 9)$ women = 22.5 women

We know that 90 women can complete the work in 1 day.

Thus, time taken by 22.5 women to complete the work = $\dfrac{1 \times 90}{22.5} = 4$ days.

The correct answer is option B.

12. 32 men and 32 boys can complete a work in 3 days.

Thus, to complete the work in 1 day, number of people required would be thrice the number

= 32×3 men and 32×3 boys

= 96 men and 96 boys

6 men and 24 boys can complete a work in 8 days.

Thus, to complete the work in 1 day, number of people required would be eight times the number

= 6×8 men and 24×8 boys

= 48 men and 192 boys

Thus as the amount of work done is same, we have:

96 men + 96 boys $\equiv$ 48 men + 192 boys

=> 48 men ≡ 96 boys

=> 1 man ≡ 2 boys

=> 6 men and 24 boys together ≡ (6 × 2 + 24) boys = 36 boys

Thus, 36 boys can complete the work in 8 days.

Again, 16 men and 4 boys together ≡ (16 × 2 + 4) boys = 36 boys

Thus, 16 men and 4 boys together can complete the work in 8 days.

The correct answer is option C.

13. Since each boy takes twice the time taken by a man, 8 boys are equivalent to $\frac{8}{2}$ = 4 men.

Thus, 8 boys and 12 men ≡ (4 + 12) men = 16 men

Thus, we have:

16 men can complete a project in 9 days

=> Time taken by 12 men to complete the project = $\frac{16 \times 9}{12}$ = 12 days

The correct answer is option D.

14. We know that Ann completes $\frac{7}{10}$ of the work in 14 days.

Ann and Joe work for 2 days to complete the remaining $\left(1 - \frac{7}{10}\right) = \frac{3}{10}$ of the work.

Fraction of the total work done by Ann in 1 day = $\left(\frac{7}{10} \times \frac{1}{14}\right) = \frac{1}{20}$

Thus, fraction of the total work done by Ann in 2 days = $2 \times \frac{1}{20} = \frac{1}{10}$

Thus, fraction of the total work done by Joe in 2 days = $\frac{3}{10} - \frac{1}{10} = \frac{1}{5}$

Thus, time taken by Joe to complete the entire work = $2 \div \left(\frac{1}{5}\right)$ = 10 days

The correct answer is option D.

15. Let the amount of water already in the boat be x liters.

Let water enter the boat at a uniform rate of w liters per hour.

Also, let each crew member remove r liters of water per hour.

Thus, we have:

- After 6 hours:

    Total water that would have been in the boat if not removed = $(x + 6w)$ liters

    Total water removed by the 5 crew members = $5 \times 6 \times r = 30r$ liters

    $=> x + 6w = 30r \ldots$ (i)

- After 4 hours:

    Total water that would have been in the boat if not removed = $(x + 4w)$ liters

    Total water removed by the 6 crew members = $6 \times 4 \times r = 24r$ liters

    $=> x + 4w = 24r \ldots$ (ii)

Subtracting (ii) from (i):

$2w = 6r => w = 3r \ldots$ (iii)

$=> x + 6\,(3r) = 30r => x = 12r \ldots$ (iv)

Let the time taken by 8 crew members be t hours.

Thus, we have:

Total water that would have been in the boat if not removed = $(x + tw)$ liters

Total water removed by the 8 crew members = $8 \times t \times r = 8tr$ liters

Thus, we have:

$x + tw = 8tr$

From (iii) and (iv):

$=> 12r + 3tr = 8tr$

$=> 12r = 5tr$

$=> t = \dfrac{12}{5} = 2.4$ hours

The correct answer is option A.

16. Let the number of men present initially be x.

Thus, x men can complete the work in 40 days

$=> 1$ man can complete the work in $40x$ days $\ldots$ (i)

Also, $(x + 5)$ men can complete the work in $(40 - 10) = 30$ days

$=> 1$ man can complete the work in $30\,(x + 5)$ days ... (ii)

Thus as the amount of work completed is same, from (i) and (ii):

$40x = 30\,(x + 5)$

$=> x = 15$

The correct answer is option B.

17. Let Pete complete x units of work in 1 hour.

Thus, John completes $\dfrac{x}{2}$ units of work in $\dfrac{1}{6}$ hour

$=>$ John completes $\left(\dfrac{x}{2} \times 6\right) = 3x$ units of work in 1 hour.

Thus, Pete and John together complete $(x + 3x) = 4x$ units of work in 1 hour.

Thus, amount of work they complete in 10 hours $= (4x \times 10) = 40x$ units.

Since Pete alone completes x units in 1 hour, time he takes to complete $40x$ units of work

$= \dfrac{40x}{x} = 40$ hours

The correct answer is option E.

18. We know that Amy and Bob can complete a piece of work in 45 days and 40 days, respectively.

Part of work completed by Amy in 1 day $= \dfrac{1}{45}$

Part of work completed by Bob in 1 day $= \dfrac{1}{40}$

Let Amy leave after t days.

Thus, part of work completed by Amy and Bob in t days $= \left(\dfrac{1}{45} + \dfrac{1}{40}\right) \times t = \dfrac{17t}{360}$

The remaining work was completed by Bob in 23 days.

Part of work completed by Bob in 23 days $= \dfrac{23}{40}$

Thus, we have:

$$\frac{23}{40} + \frac{17t}{360} = 1$$

$$\Rightarrow 207 + 17t = 360$$

$$\Rightarrow 17t = 153$$

$$\Rightarrow t = 9$$

The correct answer is option C.

19. We know that 30 men completed 25% of the work in 10 days.

Thus, 30 men can complete the remaining 75% of work in $\left(10 \times \frac{75}{25}\right)$ = 30 days.

Thus, to complete the remaining work in 1 day, number of men required = $30 \times 30 = 900$

Since the total work has to be completed in 30 days, the remaining work needs to be completed in the remaining $(30 - 10) = 20$ days.

Thus, to complete the remaining work in 20 days, number of men required = $\frac{900}{20} = 45$

Thus, number of additional men required = $45 - 30 = 15$

The correct answer is option B.

20. Since Bob left 3 days before completion, Amy had worked alone for the last 3 days.

We know that Amy can complete the entire work in 30 days.

Thus, fraction of work she can completed in one day = $\frac{1}{30}$

$\Rightarrow$ Fraction of work she completed in 3 days = $3 \times \frac{1}{30} = \frac{1}{10}$

Thus, the remaining $\left(1 - \frac{1}{10}\right) = \frac{9}{10}$ of the work was completed by Amy and Bob together.

Since Bob can complete the work in 20 days, part of the work he does in 1 day = $\frac{1}{20}$

Thus, fraction of work completed by Amy and Bob in 1 day = $\left(\frac{1}{30} + \frac{1}{20}\right) = \frac{1}{12}$

Thus, time taken to complete the remaining $\frac{9}{10}$ part of the work by Amy and Bob together

$$= \frac{9}{10} \div \frac{1}{12}$$

$$= \frac{9}{10} \times 12 = 10.8$$

$$= 10\frac{4}{5} \text{ days}$$

Thus, the duration of the entire work $= 10\frac{4}{5} + 3 = 13\frac{4}{5}$ days

The correct answer is option E.

21. Let the sum of money invested at 4% rate of interest be $\$x$

Thus, the sum of money invested at 7% rate of interest $= \$(18000 - x)$

Thus, interest on $\$x$ at 4% rate of interest in 2 years

$$= \$\left(\frac{x \times 2 \times 4}{100}\right) = \$\left(\frac{8x}{100}\right)$$

Also, interest on $\$(18000 - x)$ at 7% rate of interest in 2 years

$$= \$\left(\frac{(18000 - x) \times 2 \times 7}{100}\right) = \$\left(\frac{14(18000 - x)}{100}\right)$$

Since total interest is $2100, we have:

$$\frac{8x}{100} + \frac{14(18000 - x)}{100} = 2100$$

$$=> 14 \times 18000 - 6x = 210000$$

$$=> 6x = 252000 - 210000$$

$$=> x = 7000$$

The correct answer is option C.

22. Let the sums of money invested at 10% and 20% rates of interest be $\$x$ each.

Since the difference between the interests earned after three years is between $120 and $140, we have:

$$120 < \frac{x \times 20 \times 2}{100} - \frac{x \times 10 \times 2}{100} < 140$$

$$=> 120 < \frac{20x}{100} < 140$$

$$=> 600 < x < 700$$

We need to find the difference between the amounts earned after 2 years at compound interest at the same rates as above.

Thus, the required difference

$$= x\left(1 + \frac{20}{100}\right)^2 - x\left(1 + \frac{10}{100}\right)^2 = x\left\{\left(1 + \frac{20}{100}\right)^2 - \left(1 + \frac{10}{100}\right)^2\right\}$$

$$= x\left\{\left(1 + \frac{20}{100}\right) - \left(1 + \frac{10}{100}\right)\right\}\left\{\left(1 + \frac{20}{100}\right) + \left(1 + \frac{10}{100}\right)\right\}$$

$$= x\left(\frac{10}{100}\right)\left(2 + \frac{30}{100}\right) = x(0.1 \times 2.3) = x \times 0.23$$

We know that $600 < x < 700$

Thus, the required difference is

$$600 \times 0.23 < x \times 0.23 < 700 \times 0.23$$

$$\Rightarrow 138 < x \times 0.23 < 161$$

Thus, the required difference lies between \$138 and \$161

Only option D lies in the above range.

The correct answer is option D.

23. Interest accumulated on \$$p$ at $r\%$ rate under compound interest after period of two years

$$= \$\left\{p\left(1 + \frac{r}{100}\right)^2 - p\right\}$$

$$= \$p\left\{\frac{r}{100}\left(2 + \frac{r}{100}\right)\right\}$$

Interest accumulated on \$$q$ at $(2r)\%$ rate under simple interest after period of two years

$$= \$\left(\frac{q \times 2r \times 2}{100}\right)$$

$$= \$\left(\frac{4qr}{100}\right)$$

Since the interests are equal, we have:

$$p\left\{\frac{r}{100}\left(2 + \frac{r}{100}\right)\right\} = \frac{4qr}{100}$$

$$\Rightarrow p\left(2 + \frac{r}{100}\right) = 4q$$

$$\Rightarrow q = \frac{p}{4}\left(2 + \frac{r}{100}\right)$$

The correct answer is option E.

24. Let the sums of money invested in each case be $\$x$

The interest accumulated at 10% simple interest for two years

$$= \$ \left(\frac{x \times 10 \times 2}{100} \right) = \$ \left(\frac{x}{5} \right)$$

The interest accumulated at 25% compound interest for two years

$$= \$ \left\{ x \left(1 + \frac{25}{100} \right)^2 - x \right\} = \$x \left\{ \left(1 + \frac{1}{4} \right)^2 - 1 \right\}$$

$$= \$x \left\{ \frac{1}{4} \left(2 + \frac{1}{4} \right) \right\} = \$ \left(\frac{9x}{16} \right)$$

Note: $25\% = \dfrac{25}{100} = \dfrac{1}{4}$

Since the difference between the interests is $87, we have:

$$\frac{9x}{16} - \frac{x}{5} = 87$$

$$=> \frac{45x - 16x}{80} = 87 => \frac{29x}{80} = 87$$

$$=> x = 240$$

The correct answer is option E.

25. Let the sum of money borrowed be $100x$.

Thus, the amount after 1 year $= \$ \left(100x + \dfrac{100x \times 20 \times 1}{100} \right) = \$120x$

Amount repaid at that point of time $= \$200$

Thus, amount due $= \$ (120x - 200)$

Interest accumulated on the above in 1 more year

$$= \$ \left\{ \frac{(120x - 200) \times 20 \times 1}{100} \right\} = \$ (24x - 40)$$

Thus, the amount due

$$= \$ \{ (120x - 200) + (24x - 40) \}$$

Since this is cleared after paying $200, we have:

$$(120x - 200) + (24x - 40) = 200$$

$$=> 144x = 440$$

$$=> 100x = \frac{440}{144} \times 100 \approx 3 \times 100 = 300$$

Note: $144 \times 3 = 432 \approx 440 => \dfrac{440}{144} \approx 3$ (the value is slightly greater than 3)

Thus, the actual answer should be slightly greater than $300.

The correct answer is option E.

26. Let the time for which the first sum of money is invested be t years.

Thus, the time for which the second sum of money is invested $= (t + 2)$ years.

Interest accumulated on p for t years at 6% rate of interest

$$= \$ \left(\dfrac{p \times 6 \times t}{100} \right) = \$ \left(\dfrac{6pt}{100} \right)$$

In the second scenario, the sum of money invested is $\$ \left(\dfrac{p}{3} \right)$ and the rate of interest is 12%

Interest accumulated on $\$ \left(\dfrac{p}{3} \right)$ for $(t + 2)$ years at 12% rate of interest

$$= \$ \left(\dfrac{\left(\dfrac{p}{3} \right) \times 12 \times (t + 2)}{100} \right) = \$ \left(\dfrac{4p\,(t + 2)}{100} \right)$$

Since the difference between the interests is $120, we have:

$$\dfrac{6pt}{100} - \dfrac{4p\,(t + 2)}{100} = 120 => 2pt - 8p = 12000$$

$$=> p\,(t - 4) = 6000 => t = \dfrac{6000}{p} + 4$$

Since t is an integer, p must be a factor of 6000.

Also, since $t < 7$, we have:

$$\dfrac{6000}{p} + 4 < 7 => \dfrac{6000}{p} < 3$$

$$=> p > \dfrac{6000}{3} => p > 2000$$

Thus, greater than 2000 and a factor of 6000 can only be 3000.

Thus, we have: $p = 3000$

The correct answer is option B.

27. Let the sum of money invested in either scenario be $x

The amount for $x at 20% rate for 3 years = $x\left(1 + \dfrac{20}{100}\right)^3

The amount for $x at r% rate for 2 years = $x\left(1 + \dfrac{r}{100}\right)^2

Since the amount in both the scenarios are the same, we have:

$$x\left(1 + \frac{20}{100}\right)^3 = x\left(1 + \frac{r}{100}\right)^2$$

$$=> \left(1 + \frac{r}{100}\right)^2 = \left(1 + \frac{20}{100}\right)^3 = \frac{6}{5} \times \left(\frac{6}{5}\right)^2 = 1.2 \times \left(\frac{6}{5}\right)^2$$

Taking square root on both sides:

$$\left(1 + \frac{r}{100}\right) = \sqrt{1.2} \times \left(\frac{6}{5}\right) = 1.1 \times 1.2 = 1.32$$

$$=> \frac{r}{100} = 0.32$$

$$=> r = 32$$

The correct answer is option C.

28. Let the rates of interest in each account be r%

Let her investments for each account be $x

Interest earned on $x at r% simple interest after 2 years = $\left(\dfrac{2xr}{100}\right)$

Thus, we have:

$$\frac{2xr}{100} = 180 => \frac{xr}{100} = 90 \ldots (i)$$

Interest earned on $x at r% compound interest after 2 years = $x\left(\left(1 + \dfrac{r}{100}\right)^2 - 1\right)$

Thus, we have:

$$x\left\{\left(1 + \frac{r}{100}\right)^2 - 1\right\} = 189$$

$$=> x\left(\frac{r}{100}\right)\left(2 + \frac{r}{100}\right) = 189$$

$$=> \frac{xr}{100}\left(2 + \frac{r}{100}\right) = 189$$

Thus, using (i), we have:

$$\Rightarrow 90 \left(2 + \frac{r}{100}\right) = 189$$

$$\Rightarrow 2 + \frac{r}{100} = \frac{189}{90} = 2.1$$

$$\Rightarrow \frac{r}{100} = 0.1$$

$$\Rightarrow r = 10$$

Thus, from (i):

$$\frac{x \times 10}{100} = 90$$

$$\Rightarrow x = 900$$

Thus, Amy's total investment = $ (x + x) = $1800

The correct answer is option E.

Alternate approach:

Simple interest after 2 years is $180

=> Simple interest every year is $90

Since compound interest after 2 years is $189 and compound interest for the first year is the same as the simple interest every year, we have:

Compound interest for the second year is $189 - $90 = $99

Thus, there is a 10% increase in the compound interest from the first year to the second year.

Thus, rate of interest is 10%

Since simple interest every year is $90, we have:

10% of the investment under simple interest is $90

Thus, the investment under simple interest is $(90 × 10) = $900

Since investment under simple interest and compound interest is the same, we have:

Total investment = $900 + $900 = $1800

29. Let the amount invested be $x

Let the rate of interest be r%

Thus, the amount in the beginning of the third year, i.e. after 2 years

$$= \$x\left(1 + \frac{r}{100}\right)^2 = \$1200 \ldots \text{(i)}$$

The amount in the beginning of the fourth year, i.e. after 3 years

$$= \$x\left(1 + \frac{r}{100}\right)^3 = \$1440 \ldots \text{(ii)}$$

Dividing (ii) by (i):

$$\frac{x\left(1 + \dfrac{r}{100}\right)^3}{x\left(1 + \dfrac{r}{100}\right)^2} = \frac{1440}{1200}$$

$$=> \left(1 + \frac{r}{100}\right) = \frac{6}{5}$$

$$=> \frac{r}{100} = \frac{1}{5} => r = 20$$

Thus, from (i):

$$x\left(1 + \frac{20}{100}\right)^2 = 1200$$

$$=> x = 1200 \times \left(\frac{5}{6}\right)^2 = 1200 \times \frac{5}{6} \times \frac{5}{6} = \frac{2500}{3} = 833.3$$

$$=> x = 830 \text{ (After rounding to the nearest tens)}$$

The correct answer is option D.

30.   Let the rate of interest be $r\%$

Thus, the amount after 6 years $= \$2000\left(1 + \dfrac{r}{100}\right)^6$

Thus, we have:

$$2000\left(1 + \frac{r}{100}\right)^6 = 8000$$

$$=> \left(1 + \frac{r}{100}\right)^6 = 4$$

Taking square root on both sides:

$$\left(1 + \frac{r}{100}\right)^3 = 2$$

$$=> 1 + \frac{r}{100} = \sqrt[3]{2} = 1.25$$

$$=> r = 25$$

The correct answer is option B.

31. After replacing 2 boys, aged 15 years and 18 years, by three other boys, the average of the group reduces by 1 year.

Let the initial average age of the group be x years.

Thus, total age of the 12 boys = $12x$ years.

The total age of the group of 10 boys after the 2 boys are removed from the group

$= 12x - 15 - 18 = (12x - 33)$ years

Let the average age of the three new boys be y years.

Thus, total age of the 3 boys = $3y$ years

Thus, after these 3 boys join the group, the total age of the group of 13 boys

$= (12x - 33 + 3y)$ years

Since the average age of the group reduces by 1 year, we have:

$\dfrac{12x - 33 + 3y}{13} = x - 1$

$=> 12x - 33 + 3y = 13x - 13$

$=> 3y = x + 20$

$=> y = \dfrac{x + 20}{3} \dots (i)$

We know that the initial average age of the boys in the group lies between 12 and 15 years, inclusive.

Thus, we have: $12 \leq x \leq 15$

Thus, from (i), the only integer value of y occurs if $x = 13$

Thus, the value of $y = \dfrac{13 + 20}{3} = 11$

The correct answer is option C.

32. Let the population at the beginning of the first decade be 100.

Thus, the population after the first decade, after a 20% increase = 120% of 100 = 120

The population after the second decade, after a 25% increase = 125% of 120 = 150

The population after the third decade, after a 10% increase = 110% of 150 = 165

Thus, the overall percent increase in population after 3 decades

$$= \frac{165 - 100}{100} \times 100 = 65\%$$

Thus, the simple average rate of increase in population per decade

$$= \frac{65}{3}\% = 21.7\%$$

The correct answer is option B.

33. Let the number of students in the teams A, B, C, and D be a, b, c and d.

Since there are 40 students, we have:

$a + b + c + d = 40 \ldots$ (i)

We know that the teams, A, B, C and D, have average weights of 30 kg, 35 kg, 40 kg and 50 kg, respectively.

Since the average of all students taken together is 40 years, we have:

$$\frac{30a + 35b + 40c + 50d}{a + b + c + d} = 40$$

$=> 30a + 35b + 40c + 50d = 40a + 40b + 40c + 40d$

$=> 2a + b = 2d$

$=> b = 2\,(d - a) \ldots$ (ii)

We know that each team must have at least 2 members.

Also, we need to maximize the value of c, thus we need to minimize the values of a, b and d.

Since $a = b = d = 2$ does not satisfy, we increase the value of d to 3, keeping $a = 2$

$=> b = 2\,(3 - 2) = 2$

Thus, the smallest possible values of a, b and d are:

$a = 2, b = 2$ and $d = 3$

Thus, from (i), we have:

$c = 40 - (a + b + d) = 40 - 7 = 33$

The correct answer is option D.

34. Total age of the 7 members having average age of 25 years = $7 \times 25 = 175$ years

We know that the youngest member is 4 years old.

Thus, when the youngest member was born, i.e. 4 years ago, the age of each member would reduce by 4 years.

Thus, the total age would reduce by $7 \times 4 = 28$ years.

Thus, the total age of the $7 - 1 = 6$ members of the family

$= 175 - 28 = 147$ years

Thus, average age of the members of the family

$= \dfrac{147}{6} = 24.5$ years

The correct answer is option D.

35. Let the price of the chair, table, cot and bookshelf be a, b, c and d, respectively.

Since the average price of a chair, a table, and a cot is $70, we have:

$\dfrac{a + b + c}{3} = 70$

$=> a + b + c = 210 \ldots \text{(i)}$

Since the average price of the table, the cot and a bookshelf is $85, we have:

$\dfrac{b + c + d}{3} = 85$

$=> b + c + d = 255 \ldots \text{(ii)}$

Subtracting (i) from (ii):

$d - a = 45$

Since $d = 70$, we have:

$a = d - 45 = 25$

The correct answer is option A.

36. We know that for $\frac{1}{4}$ of the people, the salary increase was 50% on a base salary of $3000 and for the remaining $\dfrac{3}{4}$ of the people, the salary increase was 20% on a base salary of $1800.

Let the number of friends be $4n$.

After increase in salaries, we have:

Average salary of n friends having 50% increase in salary $= \$\left(\dfrac{150 \times 3000}{100}\right) = \$4500$.

Average salary of $3n$ friends having 20% increase in salary $= \$\left(\dfrac{120 \times 1800}{100}\right) = \$2160$.

Thus, average salary of the entire group

$$= \dfrac{n \times 4500 + 3n \times 2160}{4n} = \$2745$$

Note: Here, we could have done without the use of n (since n cancels out eventually) and instead we could have worked assuming only 4 friends.

The correct answer is option D.

Alternate approach:

Let there be 4 friends.

$=>$ Number of managers $= \dfrac{1}{4} \times 4 = 1$

$=>$ Number of supervisors $= \dfrac{3}{4} \times 4 = 3$

Thus, increased average salary of managers $= 1 \times (3000 + 50\% \text{ of } 3000) = \$4500$

Similarly, increased average salary of supervisors $= 3 \times (1800 + 20\% \text{ of } 1800) = \$2160$

Thus, average salary of the entire group

$$= \dfrac{1 \times 4500 + 3 \times 2160}{4} = \$2745$$

37. Ratio of number of students in groups A and B $= 2 : 3$

Number of students in group A $= 50\left(\dfrac{2}{2+3}\right) = 20$

Number of students in group B $= 50\left(\dfrac{3}{2+3}\right) = 30$

Let the average weight of students in groups A and B be a kg and b kg, respectively.

Since the average weight of all students is 40 kg, we have:

$$\dfrac{20a + 30b}{20 + 30} = 40$$

$$=> 2a + 3b = 200 \ldots \text{(i)}$$

Also, the average weight of the students in group A is 5 kg less than that of the other group.

Thus, we have:

$a = b - 5 \ldots$ (ii)

Thus, from (i) and (ii), we have:

$2(b - 5) + 3b = 200 \Rightarrow b = 42 \Rightarrow a = 37$

When Joe moves from group B to group A, the average weight of the students in either group becomes the same. Since the average weight of all students is 40 kg, after Joe shifts, the average weight of each group must become equal to the overall average, i.e. 40 kg.

Working with group A:

Total weight of 20 students in group A having an average weight of 37 kg

$= 20 \times 37 = 740$ kg

After Joe shifts to group A, number of students in group A $= 21$

Total weight of 21 students having an average weight of 40 kg $= 21 \times 40 = 840$ kg

Thus, Joe's weight $= 840 - 740 = 100$ kg

The correct answer is option E.

38. Let the average contribution of all 8 friends be $\$x$

Contribution from 7 friends $= \$(120 \times 7) = \$840$

Contribution of the last friend $= \$(x + 21)$

Thus, we have:

$840 + (x + 21) = 8x$

$\Rightarrow 7x = 861$

$\Rightarrow x = 123$

Thus, cost of the camera $= \$(8 \times 123) = \$984$

The correct answer is option E.

39. Let the average salary of junior managers be $x

Thus, the average salary of senior managers = $ $(x + 4500)$

We know that there are 80 junior managers and 100 senior managers, i.e. total 180 employees.

Thus, combined salary of all junior managers = $ $(80x)$

Also, combined salary of all senior managers = $ $(100\,(x + 4500))$

Thus, combined salary of all junior and senior managers = $ $\{80x + 100\,(x + 4500)\}$

Thus, average salary of all junior and senior managers = $ $\left\{\dfrac{80x + 100\,(x + 4500)}{180}\right\}$

Thus, required difference

$$= \$ \left\{\frac{80x + 100\,(x + 4500)}{180} - x\right\} = \$ \left\{\frac{80x + 100\,(x + 4500) - 180x}{180}\right\}$$
$$= \$ \left(\frac{4500 \times 100}{180}\right) = \$2500$$

The correct answer is option C.

Alternate approach:

We can assume any value for the average salary for the junior managers. The actual value chosen is irrelevant, since depending on this value, all other values would increase or decrease by the same amount, resulting in the required 'DIFFERENCE' to remain the same.

Thus, to simplify calculations, let us assume the average salary of junior managers be '0'

Thus, the average salary of senior managers = $4500

We know that there are 80 junior managers and 100 senior managers, i.e. total 180 employees.

Thus, combined salary of all junior managers is '0'.

Also, combined salary of all senior managers = $ (100×4500)

Thus, combined salary of all junior and senior managers = $450000

Thus, average salary of all junior and senior managers = $ $\left(\dfrac{450000}{180}\right) = \$2500$

Thus, required difference = $2500

40. The prices of each laptop and each mobile are $1200 and $900, respectively.

Total price of all items on Tuesday morning = $(1080 × 20) = $21600

We know that only laptops were sold on Tuesday.

Let the number of laptops sold be x.

Thus, reduction in total price of all items = $ $(1200x)$

Thus, total price of all items = $ $(21600 - 1200x)$

Number of items left = $(20 - x)$

Since the final average price was $1000, we have:

$1000(20 - x) = 21600 - 1200x$

$=> 200x = 1600$

$=> x = 8$

The correct answer is option B.

41. Distance travelled by the first train at 65 miles per hour in 14 hours = $65 \times 14 = 910$ miles

Since the distance between the two trains is 1960 miles and they travel in opposite directions, the sum of the distances covered by the two trains equals the distance between them.

Thus, distance travelled by the second train = 1960 – 910 = 1050 miles.

Since the speed of the second train is 105 miles per hour, time taken to travel 1050 miles $= \dfrac{1050}{105} = 10$ hours

Thus, the second train started 14 – 10 = 4 hours after the first train started.

The correct answer is option A.

42. Let the total distance be d miles.

Thus, his speed for $\frac{d}{3}$ miles is 50 miles per hour and his speed for the remaining $\frac{2d}{3}$ miles is 20 miles per hour.

Since the total time taken is 4 hours and 48 minutes, i.e. $4\frac{48}{60} = 4\frac{4}{5}$ hours, we have:

$$\frac{\frac{d}{3}}{50} + \frac{\frac{2d}{3}}{20} = 4\frac{4}{5}$$

$$\Rightarrow \frac{d}{150} + \frac{d}{30} = \frac{24}{5} \Rightarrow \frac{6d}{150} = \frac{24}{5}$$

$$\Rightarrow d = 120$$

The correct answer is option C.

43. Let the speed of the first train be x miles per hour.

Thus, the speed of the second train $= (x + 20)$ miles per hour.

In the time from 1:00 pm to 9:00 pm, i.e. 8 hours, the distance travelled by the first train

$= 8x$ miles

In the time from 5:00 pm to 9:00 pm, i.e. 4 hours, the distance travelled by the second train

$= 4(x + 20)$ miles

Since the second train started 20 miles behind LA and caught up with the first train at 9:00 pm, the distance travelled by the second train is 20 miles greater than the distance travelled by the first train.

Thus, we have:

$4(x + 20) = 8x + 20$

$\Rightarrow 4x = 60$

$\Rightarrow x = 15$

Thus, the speed of the second train $= x + 20 = 35$ miles per hour

The correct answer is option D.

44. Ratio of distances $= 6 : 4 : 5$

Ratio of speeds $= 2 : 3 : 5$

Thus, ratio of time taken $= \frac{6}{2} : \frac{4}{3} : \frac{5}{5} = 3 : \frac{4}{3} : 1$

Thus, let the actual times taken be $3x$, $\frac{4}{3}x$ and x hours, respectively.

Since the total time taken is 8 hours, we have:

$$3x + \frac{4}{3}x + x = 8 => \frac{16}{3}x = 8$$

$$=> x = \frac{3}{2}$$

The distances, in miles, travelled are:

$$\frac{6}{6+4+5} \times 150 = 60; \quad \frac{4}{6+4+5} \times 150 = 40; \quad \frac{5}{6+4+5} \times 150 = 50$$

The corresponding times, in hours, taken are:

$$3x = \frac{9}{2}; \quad \frac{4}{3}x = 2; \quad x = \frac{3}{2}$$

Thus, the corresponding speeds, in miles per hour, are:

$$\frac{60}{\frac{9}{2}} = \frac{40}{3} = 13.33; \quad \frac{40}{2} = 20; \quad \frac{50}{\frac{3}{2}} = \frac{100}{3} = 33.33$$

Thus, the maximum speed is $\frac{100}{3}$ miles per hour.

Thus, the time taken if the entire distance is covered at this speed

$$= \frac{150}{\frac{100}{3}} = 4.5 \text{ hours}$$

The correct answer is option C.

Alternate approach:

Distance	6	4	5	
Original speed	2	3	5	
Original time (Distance/speed)	3	$\frac{4}{3}$	1	Total time = $3 + \frac{4}{3} + 1 = \frac{16}{3}$
				Taking maximum speed (5)
New speed	5	5	5	
New time	$\frac{6}{5}$	$\frac{4}{5}$	1	Total time = $\frac{6}{5} + \frac{4}{5} + 1 = 3$

Thus, if the original time is $\frac{16}{3}$, the new time is 3

=> If the original time is 8 hours, the new time

$$= \frac{3}{\left(\frac{16}{3}\right)} \times 8 = \frac{9}{16} \times 8$$

$$= \frac{9}{2} = 4.5 \text{ hours}$$

45. Speed over the first d miles = x miles per hour

Thus, time taken = $\left(\frac{d}{x}\right)$ hours

Speed over the last 150% of $d = \frac{3d}{2}$ miles is 120% of $x = \frac{6x}{5}$ miles per hour

Thus, time taken = $\frac{\left(\frac{3d}{2}\right)}{\left(\frac{6x}{5}\right)} = \frac{5}{4}\left(\frac{d}{x}\right)$ hours

Thus, total time = $\left(\frac{d}{x}\right) + \frac{5}{4}\left(\frac{d}{x}\right) = \frac{9}{4}\left(\frac{d}{x}\right)$ hours ... (i)

Total distance travelled = $d + \frac{3d}{2} = \frac{5d}{2}$ miles

Thus, if the boy travelled at x miles per hour, time taken = $\frac{5}{2}\left(\frac{d}{x}\right)$ hours ... (ii)

Thus, required ratio of the time taken

$$= \frac{9}{4}\left(\frac{d}{x}\right) : \frac{5}{2}\left(\frac{d}{x}\right) = 9 : 10$$

The correct answer is option D.

Alternate approach:

We can assume any suitable value of x and d since the final answer does not depend on those values.

Let $x = 50$ miles per hour and $d = 100$ miles.

Thus, time taken over the first d miles = $\frac{100}{50} = 2$ hours

Remaining distance = 150% of 100 = 150 miles

Speed over the remaining distance = 120% of 50 = 60 miles per hour

Thus, time taken for the remaining distance = $\frac{150}{60} = 2.5$ hours

Thus, total time = 2 + 2.5 = 4.5 hours

Total distance = 100 + 150 = 250 miles

Had the boy travelled the entire distance at 50 miles per hour, time taken = $\dfrac{250}{50} = 5$ hours

Thus, required ratio = 4.5 : 5 = 9 : 10

46. Let the actual speed of the car be x miles per hour

Distance travelled = 360 miles

Time taken to cover the distance = $\left(\dfrac{360}{x}\right)$ hours

New speed of the car = $(x - 4)$ miles per hour

Thus, time taken to cover 360 miles = $\left(\dfrac{360}{x - 4}\right)$ hours

Since the time taken in the second case was 3 hours greater than in the first case, we have:

$$\dfrac{360}{x - 4} - \dfrac{360}{x} = 3$$
$$=> \dfrac{360\left\{x - (x - 4)\right\}}{(x - 4)\,x} = 3$$
$$=> x^2 - 4x - 480 = 0$$
$$=> (x - 24)\,(x + 20) = 0$$
$$=> x = 24 \text{ (Since the speed must be positive, } x \neq -20)$$

The correct answer is option D.

47. Time taken to cover x miles at 5 miles per hour = $\left(\dfrac{x}{5}\right)$ hours

Time taken to cover another 10 miles at 10 miles per hour = 1 hour

Thus, total time taken = $\left(\dfrac{x}{5} + 1\right)$ hours

Total distance travelled = $(x + 10)$ miles

Thus, time taken had he travelled throughout at 10 miles per hour

$$= \left(\dfrac{x + 10}{10}\right) = \left(\dfrac{x}{10} + 1\right) \text{ hours}$$

Thus, the required percent difference

$$= \frac{\left(\dfrac{x}{5} + 1\right) - \left(\dfrac{x}{10} + 1\right)}{\left(\dfrac{x}{10} + 1\right)} \times 100\%$$

$$= 100\left(\frac{x}{x + 10}\right)\%$$

Thus, we have:

- If $x = 1$ (smallest value)

   Required percent difference $= 100 \times \left(\dfrac{1}{11}\right) = 9.09\%$

- If $x = 10$ (largest value)

   Required percent difference $= 100 \times \left(\dfrac{10}{20}\right) = 50\%$

Thus, the required percent difference must lie between 9.09% and 50%.

Only option B satisfies the above condition.

The correct answer is option B.

Alternate approach:

Let us assume that $x = 10$

So in the original scenario, the man travelled 10 km @ 5 km/hr and another 10 km @ 10 km/hr speeds.

Thus, total time travelled $= \dfrac{10}{5} + \dfrac{10}{10} = 2 + 1 = 3$ hrs

Total time for the revised scenario $= \dfrac{20}{10} = 2$ hrs

Thus, the required percent difference

$$= \frac{3 - 2}{2} \times 100\% = 50\%$$

Since $1 \leq x \leq 10$, the answers which are less or equal to 50% may be correct. But there are two qualifying options: A (8%) and B (23%).

Need we solve the question with another approach to eliminate one of the options? The answer is NO! There is no need to do so, since this is a PS question and only one option can be correct. If option A (8%) is correct, it is for sure that option B (23%) is also correct; however, if option B (23%) is correct, it is NOT certain that option A (8%) is also correct. Thus, the best bet is option B. It can be intuited that 8% would qualify had $x < 1$.

48. Part of the work done by A in 1 hour = $\dfrac{1}{15}$

Part of the work done by B in 1 hour = $\dfrac{1}{18}$

Part of the work completed by A alone in 6 hours = $\dfrac{1}{15} \times 6 = \dfrac{2}{5}$

Part of the work completed by A and B together in next 3 hours = $\left(\dfrac{1}{15} + \dfrac{1}{18}\right) \times 3 = \dfrac{11}{30}$

Thus, part of the work remaining = $1 - \left(\dfrac{2}{5} + \dfrac{11}{30}\right) = \dfrac{7}{30}$

Thus, time taken by B to complete the remaining work alone

$= \dfrac{\left(\dfrac{7}{30}\right)}{\left(\dfrac{1}{18}\right)} = \dfrac{7}{30} \times 18 = 4\dfrac{1}{5}$ hours

The correct answer is option A.

49. Since A and B take 12 hours to fill the tank, part of the tank filled by (A + B) in 1 hour = $\dfrac{1}{12}$

Since A and C take 15 hours to fill the tank, part of the tank filled by (A + C) in 1 hour = $\dfrac{1}{15}$

Since B and C take 20 hours to fill the tank, part of the tank filled by (B + C) in 1 hour = $\dfrac{1}{20}$

Adding the above three results, we have:

Part of the tank filled by 2 (A + B + C) in 1 hour = $\dfrac{1}{12} + \dfrac{1}{15} + \dfrac{1}{20} = \dfrac{1}{5}$

Thus, part of the tank filled by (A + B + C) in 1 hour = $= \dfrac{1}{2} \times \dfrac{1}{5} = \dfrac{1}{10}$

Thus, time taken to complete the work with A, B and C working together = $\dfrac{1}{\left(\dfrac{1}{10}\right)} = 10$ hours

The correct answer is option C.

50. We know that:

Time taken by A and B together to complete a work = 24 days

Time taken by C alone to complete the same work = 28 days

The pattern in which A, B and C worked to complete the work is:

A and C worked for 4 days; B and C worked for 10 days; and B worked for 4 days

=> A worked for 4 days, B worked for 14 days and C worked for 14 days

=> A and B worked for 4 days, C worked for 14 days and B worked for 14 – 4 = 10 days

Part of work completed by A and B in 4 days = $\dfrac{4}{24} = \dfrac{1}{6}$

Part of work completed by C in 14 days = $\dfrac{14}{28} = \dfrac{1}{2}$

Thus, part of work completed by B in 10 days = $1 - \left(\dfrac{1}{6} + \dfrac{1}{2} \right) = \dfrac{1}{3}$

Thus, time taken by B to complete the entire work = $\dfrac{10}{\left(\dfrac{1}{3}\right)} = 30$ days

The correct answer is option E.

51. We can represent the situation using a diagram, as shown below:

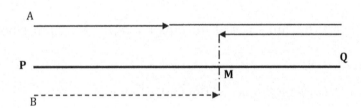

Assuming M to be the meeting point, and distance from P to M be d meters, we have:

Distance from P to Q = 200 meters

=> Distance from Q to M = (200 – d) meters

Thus, distance travelled by A = (Distance from P to Q) + (Distance from Q to M) = 200 + (200 – d)

= (400 – d) meters

Distance travelled by B = Distance from P to M

= d meters

Since both A and B travel for the same time, the ratio of the distances they cover is equal to the ratio of their speeds, given as 7 : 1.

Thus, we have:

$$\frac{400 - d}{d} = \frac{7}{1}$$

$$=> d = 50$$

The correct answer is option B.

Alternate Approach:

Both A and B travel for same amount of time. So if, B travels x distance, then A will travel $7x$ distance as the ratio of their speeds is $7 : 1$.

Total distance travelled by both of them together $= x + 7x = 8x$

According to the diagram, we see both of them together travelled $2 \times 200 = 400$ meters.

Thus, $8x = 400 => x = 50$

52. We know that Bob and Chad started at the same time. However, Chad stopped for 15 minutes on the way. Hence, Chad would have covered a distance equivalent to 15 minutes less than the distance had he not made the stop.

However, this scenario is exactly the same as if Chad had started 15 minutes after Bob had started, hence covering a distance equivalent to 15 minutes less than the distance had he stated along with Bob.

Thus, in the first 15 minutes, distance travelled by Bob at 60 miles per hour

$$= 60 \times \frac{15}{60} = 15 \text{ miles}$$

Distance remaining between Bob and Chad when Chad started his journey

$$= 150 - 15 = 135 \text{ miles}$$

Since Bob and Chad move in opposite directions at speeds of 60 miles per hour and 30 miles per hour, we have:

Relative speed $= 60 + 30 = 90$ miles per hour

Thus, time taken for Bob and Chad to meet

$$= \frac{\text{Distance}}{\text{Relative speed}} = \frac{135}{90}$$

$$= 1.5 \text{ hours}$$

In 1.5 hours, distance covered by Chad = 1.5 × 30 = 45 miles

Thus, they meet at a distance of 45 miles from point B.

The correct answer is option B.

53. We know that:

Time taken by A to complete the work = x days

Time taken by B to complete the work = kx days

Thus, part of the work completed by A and B together in 1 day

$$= \frac{1}{x} + \frac{1}{kx} = \frac{k+1}{kx}$$

Thus, time taken by A and B to complete the work = $\left(\frac{kx}{k+1}\right)$ days

We know that $\left(\frac{kx}{k+1}\right)$ is an integer.

Thus, $(k+1)$ is a factor of kx

However, k and $(k+1)$ are consecutive integers, and hence are co-prime to one another.

Thus, $(k+1)$ or a part of $(k+1)$ cannot be a factor of k.

Thus, $(k+1)$ must be a factor of x ... (i)

We also know that:

$$\frac{kx}{k+1} < 5$$

$$=> \frac{kx}{k+1} \leq 4 \ldots \text{(ii)}$$

Thus, from (i) and (ii), the possible scenarios are:

* $k = 1 => k + 1 = 2$

    $=> 2$ is a factor of x, i.e. x is an even number

    $=>$ Possible values of x are: 2, 4, 6 or 8

    $=>$ Possible values of (k, x) are: $(1, 2)$, $(1, 4)$, $(1, 6)$, $(1, 8)$

    Thus, there are four possible values of (k, x)

* $k = 2 => k + 1 = 3$

    $=> 3$ is a factor of x

=> Possible values of x are: 3 or 6

=> Possible values of (k, x) are: $(2, 3)$, $(2, 6)$

Thus, there are two possible values of (k, x)

- $k = 3 => k + 1 = 4$

    => 4 is a factor of x

    => Possible value of x is: 4

    => Possible value of (k, x) is: $(3, 4)$

    Thus, there is one possible value of (k, x)

- $k = 4 => k + 1 = 5$

    => 5 is a factor of x

    => Possible value of x is: 5

    => Possible value of (k, x) is: $(4, 5)$

    Thus, there is one possible value of (k, x)

For any higher value of k, the inequality given in (ii) is not satisfied.

Thus, the number of possible values of the ordered set of (k, x) are:

$4 + 2 + 1 + 1 = 8$

The correct answer is option D.

54. We can represent the situation using a diagram, as shown below:

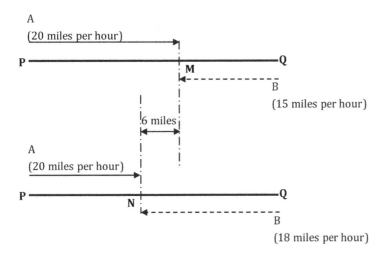

Assuming M to be the meeting point, we have:

Since in either case, A and B start simultaneously, the ratio of their distances is equal to the ratio of their speeds.

Thus, we have:

- First case: $\dfrac{PM}{QM} = \dfrac{20}{15} = \dfrac{4}{3}$

  $=> PM = \dfrac{4}{3}QM \ldots (i)$

- Second case: $\dfrac{PN}{QN} = \dfrac{20}{18} = \dfrac{10}{9}$

  $=> \dfrac{PM - 6}{QM + 6} = \dfrac{10}{9}$

Thus, from (i), we have:

$$\dfrac{\frac{4}{3}QM - 6}{QM + 6} = \dfrac{10}{9} => \dfrac{4QM - 18}{3QM + 18} = \dfrac{10}{9}$$

$$=> 36QM - 162 = 30QM + 180$$

$$=> QM = 57$$

The correct answer is option C.

Alternate Approach:

Say PM = x and MQ = y

$=> PN = x - 6$ and NQ = $y + 6$

In the original scenario:

Time taken by A to reach point M = Time taken by B to reach point M

$=> \dfrac{x}{20} = \dfrac{y}{15} => x = \dfrac{4y}{3}$

In the revised scenario:

Time taken by A to reach point N = Time taken by B to reach point N

$=> \dfrac{x - 6}{20} = \dfrac{y + 6}{18} => \dfrac{x - 6}{10} = \dfrac{y + 6}{9}$

$=> 9(x - 6) = 10(y + 6)$

$$=> 9x - 54 = 10y + 60$$

$$=> 9x = 10y + 114$$

$$=> 9 \times \frac{4y}{3} = 10y + 114$$

$$=> 12y = 10y + 114$$

$$=> 2y = 114$$

$$=> y = 57 = QM$$

55. Let the required time be t hours.

Thus, distance covered by A, running at 12 miles per hour, in t hours = $12t$ miles

Distance covered by B, running at 10 miles per hour, in t hours = $10t$ miles

We know that A completed one lap more than that completed by B.

Thus, the distance covered by A is 15 miles more than that covered by B after t hours.

Thus, we have:

$$12t - 10t = 15$$

$$=> t = 7.5$$

Note:

In 7.5 hours, distance covered by A = $7.5 \times 12 = 90$ miles = $\frac{90}{15} = 6$ laps (an integer value)

In 7.5 hours, distance covered by B = $7.5 \times 10 = 75$ miles = $\frac{75}{15} = 5$ laps (an integer value)

The difference between the numbers of laps covered by A and B = 6 - 5 = 1

The correct answer is option B.

Alternate Approach:

Since A and b are running in the same direction, their relative speed

= 12 - 10 = 2 miles/hr.

Given that A leads B by one lap or 15 miles, we have:

$$\text{Time} = \frac{\text{Distance}}{\text{Speed}} = \frac{15}{2} = 7.5 \text{ hours.}$$

56. We know that Jane always takes twice as much time to solve a data-sufficiency question as a problem-solving question.

Thus, we have:

20 problem-solving and 10 data-sufficiency ≡ 20 problem-solving and 20 problem-solving

≡ 40 problem-solving questions

Similarly, we have:

30 problem-solving and 20 data-sufficiency ≡ 30 problem-solving and 40 problem-solving

≡ 70 problem-solving questions

Thus, Jane had solved 40 problem-solving questions in the stipulated time and she wants to solve 70 problem-solving questions in the same time.

Let the time taken be t hours.

Thus, time taken per question initially = $\dfrac{t}{40}$ hours.

Time taken per question finally = $\dfrac{t}{70}$ hours.

Thus, percent reduction in time = $\dfrac{\dfrac{t}{40} - \dfrac{t}{70}}{\dfrac{t}{40}} \times 100$

$= \left(1 - \dfrac{40}{70}\right) \times 100 = \dfrac{3}{7} \times 100$

$= 42.9\%$

The correct answer is option B.

Alternatively, we can assume that the time taken be 280 hours. (LCM of 40 and 70)

Thus, time taken per question initially = $\dfrac{280}{40}$ = 7 hours.

Time taken per question finally = $\dfrac{280}{70}$ = 4 hours.

Thus, percent reduction in time

$= \dfrac{7 - 4}{7} \times 100$

$= \dfrac{3}{7} \times 100$

$= 42.9\%$

57. We know that during morning walks, Brenda takes 45 strides, each 2 feet long, per minute.

Thus, distance she covers per minute = $45 \times 2 = 90$ feet.

During going to school, Brenda's speed is 50% higher

Thus, distance she covers per minute while going to school = 150% of 90 = 135 feet.

While going to school, her each stride is 2.5 feet long.

Thus, the number of strides she takes per minute = $\dfrac{135}{2.5} = \dfrac{135 \times 2}{5} = 54$

Thus, the number of more strides she takes while going to school than during her morning walks

$= 54 - 45 = 9$

The correct answer is option A.

58. We know that:

5 servers can process 45,000 search requests per hour

$=> 1$ server in 1 hour can process $\dfrac{45000}{5} = 9000$ search requests ... (i)

The service provider needs to process 216,000 search requests in 3 hours.

Thus, the number of search requests required to be processed in 1 hour $= \dfrac{216000}{3} = 72000$

Thus, from (i), we observe that the required number of search requests processed in 1 hour is $\dfrac{72000}{9000} = 8$ times the number of search requests that can be processed by 1 server in 1 hour.

Thus, the number of servers required is 8.

However, there are already 5 servers present.

Thus, the number of additional servers required = 8 - 5 = 3.

The correct answer is option B.

59. The percent profit made by selling the final mixture at $8.40 a pound = 20%.

Thus, we have:

$(100 + 20)\%$ of Cost price of the final mixture per pound = $8.40

$\Rightarrow$ Cost price of the final mixture per pound = $\left(\dfrac{100}{120} \times 8.40 \right) = \$7$.

Let the quantity of Jamaica Blue Mountain beans used be x pounds.

Thus, on mixing x pounds of Jamaica Blue Mountain beans priced at $19.00 per pound and 8 pounds of Colombian coffee beans priced at $4.00 per pound, we get a mixture which costs $7 per pound.

Thus, we have:

$\dfrac{x \times 19 + 8 \times 4}{x + 8} = 7$

$\Rightarrow 19x + 32 = 7\,(x + 8)$

$\Rightarrow 19x + 32 = 7x + 56$

$\Rightarrow 12x = 24$

$\Rightarrow x = 2$

The correct answer is option B.

60. Since we need the expression for average speed, we can assume any suitable value of the total distance since the distance does not affect the value of the average speed.

Let the total distance be 100.

Distance travelled at 40 miles per hour

$= x\%$ of 100

$= x$

Thus, time (in hours) taken to cover the above distance

$= \dfrac{x}{40}$

Distance travelled at 60 miles per hour

$$= (100 - x)$$

Thus, time (in hours) taken to cover the above distance

$$= \frac{(100 - x)}{60}$$

Thus, average speed

$$= \frac{\text{(Total distance)}}{\text{(Total time)}}$$

$$= \frac{100}{\dfrac{x}{40} + \dfrac{(100 - x)}{60}}$$

$$= \frac{120 \times 100}{3x + 2(100 - x)}$$

$$= \frac{12000}{x + 200}$$

The correct answer is option E.

Alternate approach:

Let us plug in a value for x, calculate the average speed and identify the correct answer by substituting that value of x in each option.

Let the total distance be 100.

Let $x = 40$ (40 is the best choice since in that case, the distances would be easily divisible by the corresponding values of the speeds).

Distance travelled at 40 miles per hour

$$= 40\% \text{ of } 100 = 40$$

Thus, time (in hours) taken to cover the above distance

$$= \frac{40}{40} = 1$$

Distance travelled at 60 miles per hour

$$= (100 - 40) = 60$$

Thus, time (in hours) taken to cover the above distance

$$= \frac{60}{60} = 1$$

Thus, average speed

$$= \frac{\text{(Total distance)}}{\text{(Total time)}} = \frac{100}{1 + 1} = 50$$

Substituting $x = 40$ in each option, we get:

Option A: $\dfrac{180 - x}{2} = \dfrac{140}{2} = 70$ – Does not satisfy

Option B: $\dfrac{x + 60}{4} = \dfrac{100}{4} = 25$ – Does not satisfy

Option C: $\dfrac{300 - x}{5} = \dfrac{260}{5} = 52$ – Does not satisfy

Option D: $\dfrac{600}{115 - x} = \dfrac{600}{75} = 80$ – Does not satisfy

Option E: $\dfrac{12000}{x + 200} = \dfrac{12000}{240} = 50$ – Satisfies

61. The average cost per book for 12 books = $\$k$

Thus, the total cost of the 12 books = $\$12k$

Cost of the book removed = $\$18$

Cost of the book added = $\$42$

Thus, cost of the books on the table

$= \$(12k - 18 + 42)$

$= \$(12k + 24)$

Number of books on the table $= 12 - 1 + 1 = 12$

Thus, average cost per book on the table

$= \dfrac{\text{Total cost of all books}}{\text{Number of books}}$

$= \$\left(\dfrac{12k + 24}{12}\right)$

$= \$(k + 2)$

The correct answer is option A.

Alternate approach:

After one book costing $\$18$ was removed and one book costing $\$42$ was added, the total cost of all the books increased by $\$(42 - 18) = \$24$

Since there are 12 books, the average cost increased by $\$\dfrac{24}{12} = \$2$

Since the initial average was $\$k$, the new average = $\$(k + 2)$

62. The average score on a test taken by 10 students = x

Thus, the total score of the 10 students = $10x$

The average score of 5 of the students = 8

Thus, the total score of the 5 students = $8 \times 5 = 40$

Thus, the total score of the remaining 5 students = $10x - 40$

Thus, the average score of the remaining 5 students = $\dfrac{10x - 40}{5} = 2x - 8$

The correct answer is option A.

63. Sales tax applicable in State A

$= \$(t\% \text{ of } p)$

$= \$\left(\dfrac{pt}{100}\right)$

Thus, total cost of the computer in State A

$= \$\left(p + \dfrac{pt}{100}\right)$

$= \$\left(p\left(1 + \dfrac{t}{100}\right)\right) \ldots \text{(i)}$

Sales tax applicable in State B

$= \$(T\% \text{ of } P)$

$= \$\left(\dfrac{PT}{100}\right)$

Thus, total cost of the computer in State A

$= \$\left(P + \dfrac{PT}{100}\right)$

$= \$\left(P\left(1 + \dfrac{T}{100}\right)\right) \ldots \text{(ii)}$

From statement 1:

There is no information regarding which one between P and p is greater. – Insufficient

From statement 2:

We have:

$pt > PT$

Thus, the tax paid in State A is greater than that paid in State B.

However, this does not necessarily imply a higher total cost in State A.

For example:

(1) If $p = 100, t = 10, P = 200, T = 2$:

Here, we have: $pt = 1000 > PT = 400$

Total cost in State A = $\$\left(100\left(1 + \dfrac{10}{100}\right)\right) = \$110$

Total cost in State B = $\$\left(200\left(1 + \dfrac{2}{100}\right)\right) = \$204$

Thus, the total cost in State B is greater than that in State A.

(2) If $p = 200, t = 10, P = 100, T = 2$:

Here, we have: $pt = 2000 > PT = 200$

Total cost in State A = $\$\left(200\left(1 + \dfrac{10}{100}\right)\right) = \$220$

Total cost in State B = $\$\left(100\left(1 + \dfrac{2}{100}\right)\right) = \$102$

Thus, the total cost in State A is greater than that in State B.

Thus, the answer cannot be uniquely determined. – Insufficient

Thus, from statements 1 and 2 together:

We can observe that the two situations discussed above satisfy both conditions in statements 1 and 2. Also, no information about P and p is given.

Thus, the answer cannot be uniquely determined. – Insufficient

The correct answer is option E.

64. Calls between 5:00 am and 9:00 pm are charged at $0.40 per minute.

Calls between 9:00 pm and 5:00 am are charged at $0.25 per minute.

A call at 8:00 pm, i.e. between 5:00 am and 9:00 pm, is charged $30.00

The call charges would be $0.40 per minute from 8:00 pm to 9:00 pm, i.e. for 60 minutes, after which, the call charges would change to $0.25 per minute.

Assuming that the call does not extend till a time when the call rates are different, the duration of the call comes to be

$$= \frac{30}{0.40} = 75 \text{ minutes}$$

Since the duration is more than 60 minutes, a different call charge would be applicable for the last part of the call.

Charge for the first 60 minutes

$= \$ (60 \times 0.40)$

$= \$24.00$

Thus, the charge on a call for the last part, billed at \$0.25 per minute

$= \$(30.00 - 24.00) = \$6.00$

Thus, the duration of the last part of the call

$$= \frac{6}{0.25} = 24 \text{ minutes}$$

Thus, the total duration of the call $= (60 + 24) = 84$ minutes

We need to calculate the charge on a call of the same duration, made at 11:00 pm, i.e. between 9:00 pm and 5:00 am.

Since the duration is 84 minutes, the entire call would be at the same charge of \$0.25 per minute.

Thus, the charge on the call

$= \$ (84 \times 0.25)$

$= \$21.00$

The correct answer is option E.

Alternate approach:

We know that the first 60 minutes of the call is charged at \$0.40 per minute giving a total charge of \$ $(60 \times 0.40) = \$24.00$

The remaining amount billed $= \$ (30.00 - 24.00) = \$6.00$

For the new call, the entire duration would be charged at \$0.25 per minute.

Thus, the initial 60 minutes which had been charged at \$0.40 per minute, would be now charged at \$0.25per minute, giving a charge $= \$ (60 \times 0.25) = \$15.00$

However, the remaining part of the call would still be charged at $0.25 per minute, as before, resulting in the charge of $6.00

Thus, the total charge = $ (15.00 + 6.00) = $21.00

65. Total sales of popcorn (3 bags at $5.25 each)

= $(5.25 × 3)

= $15.75

Total sales of soda (4 at $4.50 each)

= $(4.50 × 4)

= $18.00

Total sales of candy bars (2 at $3.00 each)

= $(3.00 × 2)

= $6.00

Thus, total sales of all snacks (for every 16 admission tickets)

= $(15.75 + 18.00 + 6.00)

= $39.75

Thus, the average amount of snacks sold per ticket

$$= \$ \left(\frac{39.75}{16} \right)$$

$$= \approx \$ \left(\frac{40}{16} \right)$$

$$= \$ \left(\frac{5}{2} \right)$$

= $2.50

(Note: The actual answer would be slightly lesser than $2.50 (it actually is $2.48) since we approximated $39.75 to $40. However, we only want an approximate answer, and, $2.48 when approximated can be written as $2.50)

The correct answer is option C.

66. Let the time taken by the man while traveling by air and while traveling by train be t hours and T hours, respectively.

Since the total time is 8 hours, we have:

$T + t = 8 \ldots (i)$

The man would have saved $\frac{4}{5}$ of the time he was in train had he travelled all the way by air.

$=>$ Time saved $= \frac{4T}{5}$

Again, we know that he would reach 4 hours early had he travelled entirely by air.

Thus, the time saved is 4 hours

$=> \frac{4T}{5} = 4$

$=> T = 5$

$=> t = 8 - 5 = 3 \ldots$ using equation (i)

Had the man travelled entirely by air, he would have taken 8 – 4 = 4 hours.

Thus, speed of the man by air $= \frac{720}{4} = 180$ miles per hour.

Thus, the distance, in miles, originally travelled by the man by air

$= 180 \times t$

$= 180 \times 3 = 540$

The correct answer is option C.

67. Since we need to find the average speed, we may assume any suitable value of the distance.

Since we need to take $\frac{1}{3}$ of the distance, and also divide a part of the distance by 12, 20 and 40 (since speeds are given as 20, 12 and 40 miles per hour), it is best to assume the distance to be a multiple of 120 (LCM of 20, 12 and 40).

To be on the safer side, let us assume the distance to be 360 miles.

Distance travelled at 20 miles per hour $= \frac{1}{3} \times 360 = 120$ miles.

Thus, time taken = $\dfrac{120}{20}$ = 6 hours ... (i)

Distance left to be covered = 360 – 120 = 240 miles.

Distance travelled at 12 miles per hour = $\dfrac{1}{2}\times$Distance left to be covered = $\dfrac{1}{2}\times 240 = 120$ miles.

Thus, time taken = $\dfrac{120}{12}$ = 10 hours ... (ii)

Distance left to be covered = 240 – 120 = 120 miles.

This distance is travelled at 40 miles per hour.

Thus, time taken = $\dfrac{120}{40}$ = 3 hours ... (ii)

Thus, from (i), (ii) and (iii), we have:

Total time taken = 6 + 10 + 3 = 19 hours.

Thus, average speed

$$= \frac{\text{Total distance}}{\text{Total time}}$$
$$= \frac{360}{19}$$
$$\frac{360}{19} > \frac{360}{20} = 18$$
$$\frac{360}{19} < \frac{361}{19} = 19$$

Thus, the actual value of the average speed will be between 18 and 19.

The correct answer is option C.

68. Number of floors Jane needs to cover = x.

Thus, time taken to walk down the steps for all x floors taking 30 seconds per floor

= $30x$ seconds

Time taken to wait for the elevator and ride for x floors taking 2 seconds per floor

= 7 minutes + $2x$ seconds

= $(420 + 2x)$ seconds

Thus, we have:

$30x = 420 + 2x$

$=> x = \dfrac{420}{28} = 15$

The correct answer is option D.

69. Distance covered by Mary in 15 minutes traveling at 50 miles per hour

$= 50 \times \dfrac{15}{60}$

$= 12.5$ miles

Thus, when Paul crossed the gas station, the distance between Mary and Paul = 12.5 miles.

Since both Mary and Paul are traveling in the same direction, their relative speed

= Speed of Paul – Speed of Mary

$= 60 - 50 = 10$ miles per hour.

Thus, time taken by Paul to catch up with Mary

$= \dfrac{\text{Distance between them}}{\text{Relative speed}}$

$= \dfrac{12.5}{10}$

$= 1.25$ hours

$= 1.25 \times 60$ minutes

$= 75$ minutes

The correct answer is option D.

70. At 10:00 am, the man and the bus were at the same point (since the man overtook the bus), say point Z.

The man reached City Y at 2:00 pm.

Thus, time taken by the man to reach City Y from point Z

= Time difference between 2:00 pm and 10:00 am

= 4 hours

On the way back let the man meets the bus at 3:00 pm at point W.

Thus, the time taken by the bus to travel from point Z to point W

= Time difference between 3:00 pm and 10:00 am

= 5 hours

The above situation can be represented in the diagram below:

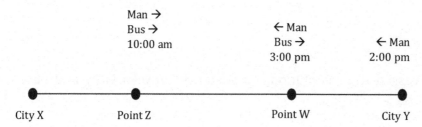

Thus, from the diagram above, we can say that:

The distance ZY is equivalent to 4 hours travel of the man ...(i)

The distance WY is equivalent to 1 hour travel of the man ...(ii)

From (i) and (ii):

The distance WZ is equivalent to (4 − 1) = 3 hours travel of the man ...(iii)

The distance WZ is equivalent to 5 hours travel of the bus ...(iv)

Thus, from (iii) and (iv), we have:

3 hours travel of the man ≡ 5 hours travel of the bus

=> 1 hour travel of the man (dist. WY) ≡ $\frac{5}{3}$ hour travel of the bus (dist. WY)

Thus, time taken by the bus to travel from point W to City Y

= $\frac{5}{3}$ hours = $1\frac{2}{3}$ hours

= 1 hour 40 minutes

Thus, the bus reached City Y 1 hour 40 minutes after 3:00 pm

= 4:40 pm

The correct answer is option E.

71.   Speed of Jack = 3 miles per hour.

Distance covered by Jack (before Bob started walking) in 2 hours = 3 × 2 = 6 miles.

Thus, total distance between Jack and Bob = 6 miles.

Speed of Bob = 5 miles per hour.

Relative speed (in same direction) of Jack and Bob = 5 – 3 = 2 miles per hour.

Thus, time taken for them to meet

$$= \frac{\text{Distance}}{\text{Relative speed}}$$

$$= \frac{6}{2}$$

$$= 3 \text{ hours}$$

Distance covered by Bob in these 3 hours = 3 × 5 = 15 miles.

Thus, the number of miles before Q where Bob overtook Jack

$$= 25 - 15$$

$$= 10$$

The correct answer is option B.

72.   Time taken by the first inlet pipe to fill the tank to $\frac{1}{2}$ of capacity = 3 hours.

=> Fraction of the tank filled by the first inlet pipe in 1 hour = $\frac{1}{2} \times \frac{1}{3} = \frac{1}{6}$

Time taken by the second inlet pipe to fill the tank to $\frac{2}{3}$ of capacity = 6 hours.

=> Fraction of the tank filled by the second inlet pipe in 1 hour = $\frac{2}{3} \times \frac{1}{6} = \frac{1}{9}$

Thus, fraction of the tank filled in 1 hour by both pipes working together

$$= \frac{1}{6} + \frac{1}{9}$$

$$= \frac{5}{18}$$

=> Time taken by both pipes to fill the tank to capacity

$$= \frac{1}{\left(\frac{5}{18}\right)} = \frac{18}{5}$$

$$= 3.6 \text{ hours}$$

The correct answer is option B.

73. Let machine Y takes a days to produce w widgets.

Thus, machine X takes $(a + 2)$ days to produce w widgets.

Thus, total widgets produced by machines X and Y in 1 day

$$= \frac{w}{a} + \frac{w}{a + 2}$$

$$= w \left(\frac{1}{a} + \frac{1}{a + 2} \right)$$

$$= \frac{w (2a + 2)}{a (a + 2)}$$

Thus, total widgets produced by machines X and Y in 3 days

$$= \frac{3w (2a + 2)}{a (a + 2)}$$

Thus, we have:

$$\frac{3w (2a + 2)}{a (a + 2)} = \frac{5}{4} w$$

$$=> \frac{3 (2a + 2)}{a (a + 2)} = \frac{5}{4}$$

$$=> 24a + 24 = 5a^2 + 10a$$

$$=> 5a^2 - 14a - 24 = 0$$

$$=> 5a^2 - 20a + 6a - 24 = 0$$

$$=> (a - 4)(5a + 6) = 0$$

Since a is positive, we have:

$$a = 4$$

Thus, time taken by machine X to produce w widgets $= (a + 2) = 6$ days

Thus, time taken by machine X to produce $2w$ widgets $= 2 \times 6 = 12$ days

The correct answer is option E.

74. Let the quantity of the sample be x.

Thus, amount of impurity present

$= 10\%$ of x

$$= \frac{10}{100} \times x$$

$$= \frac{x}{10}$$

After each purification process, the amount of impurity reduces by 60%.

Let the required number of times the purification has to be done = n.

Thus, the final amount of impurity

$$= \frac{x}{10} \times \left(1 - \frac{60}{100}\right)^n$$

Thus, we have:

$$\frac{x}{10} \times \left(1 - \frac{60}{100}\right)^n \leq 1\% \text{ of } x$$

$$=> \frac{x}{10} \times \left(1 - \frac{60}{100}\right)^n \leq \frac{x}{100}$$

$$=> \left(\frac{2}{5}\right)^n \leq \frac{1}{10}$$

$$=> \left(\frac{2 \times 2}{5 \times 2}\right)^n \leq \frac{1}{10}$$

$$=> \left(\frac{4}{10}\right)^n \leq \frac{1}{10}$$

$$=> 4^n \leq 10^{(n-1)}$$

As per the answer options, for $n = 2$, $4^2 = 16 \nleq 10^1$ – Does not satisfy

For $n = 3$, $4^3 \leq 10^2$ => $64 \leq 100$ – Satisfies

The correct answer is option B.

75. Under compound interest, if a sum of money P is invested at $r\%$ annual rate of interest for t years, the amount A is given by:

$$A = P\left(1 + \frac{r}{100}\right)^t$$

Thus, the interest accumulated

$$= A - P$$

$$= P\left(1 + \frac{r}{100}\right)^t - P$$

For Tim:

$P = \$1000$, $r = 10\%$, $t = 2$ years

$$\Rightarrow \text{Interest} = \$\left(1000\left(1 + \frac{10}{100}\right)^2 - 1000\right)$$

$$= \$\left(1000\left(\frac{11}{10} \times \frac{11}{10}\right) - 1000\right)$$

$$= \$(10 \times 121 - 1000)$$

$$= \$(1210 - 1000)$$

$$= \$210$$

For Lana:

$P = \$2000$, $r = 5\%$, $t = 2$ years

$$\Rightarrow \text{Interest} = \$\left(2000\left(1 + \frac{5}{100}\right)^2 - 2000\right)$$

$$= \$\left(2000\left(\frac{21}{20} \times \frac{21}{20}\right) - 2000\right)$$

$$= \$(5 \times 441 - 2000)$$

$$= \$(2205 - 2000)$$

$$= \$205$$

Thus, the different in total interest accumulated after two years

$$= \$(210 - 205)$$

$$= \$5$$

The correct answer is option A.

76. Calls between 5:00 am and 9:00 pm are charged at $0.40 per minute.

Calls between 9:00 pm and 5:00 am are charged at $0.25 per minute.

A call at 1:00 pm, i.e. between 5:00 am and 9:00 pm, is charged $10.00

The duration of the call $= \dfrac{10}{0.40} = 25$ minutes

We find that the duration of the call does not extend till a time when the call rates are different.

Thus, the charge on a call of the same duration, made at 11:00 pm, i.e. between 9:00 pm and 5:00 am with charge $0.25 per minute.

$= \$ \, (0.25 \times 25)$

$= \$6.25$

Alternate approach:

We can say that the rate of charge for the calls between 9:00 pm and 5:00 am is $\dfrac{25}{40} = \dfrac{5}{8}$ of the rate of charge for the calls between 5:00 am and 9:00 pm.

Thus, the charge on a call of the same duration, made at 11:00 pm, i.e. between 9:00 pm and 5:00 am

$= \$ \left(\dfrac{5}{8} \times 10 \right) = \$6.25$

The correct answer is option B.

5.2   Data Sufficiency

77. We need to determine whether b the average of the four numbers a, b, c and d

$$=> b = \frac{a + b + c + d}{4}$$

$$=> 3b = a + c + d \ldots (i)$$

From statement 1:

The average of c and d is $\frac{3b}{2}$

$$=> \frac{c + d}{2} = \frac{3b}{2}$$

$$=> c + d = 3b$$

Thus, (i) would be valid only if $a = 0$.

However, it is not possible since a is a positive number.

Thus, we get a specific answer that b cannot be the average of the four numbers a, b, c and d. – Sufficient

From statement 2:

The average of a, b and c is b

$$=> \frac{a + b + c}{3} = b$$

$$=> a + b + c = 3b$$

$$=> a + c = 2b$$

Thus, (i) would be valid only if $d = b$.

However, it is not possible since $d > b$.

Thus, again we get a specific answer that b cannot be the average of the four numbers a, b, c and d. – Sufficient

The correct answer is option D.

78. Let the number of students originally in the class be n.

Let the average age of the students originally in the class be a years.

Thus, the total age of the students originally in the class = na years.

Let the number of students who join the class be m.

Let the average age of the students who join the class be b years.

Thus, the total age of the students who join the class = mb years.

Total age of all the students = $(na + mb)$ years.

Total number of students = $(n + m)$

Thus, the final average age of the students in the class = $\left(\dfrac{na + mb}{n + m} \right)$ years.

Since the average age of the class decreases by one year, we have:

$\dfrac{na + mb}{n + m} = a - 1$

$=> na + mb = na + ma - n - m$

$=> m(a - b - 1) = n \ldots \text{(i)}$

We need to determine the value of a.

From statement 1:

We have: $b = 15$

However, the value of a cannot be determined since the values of m and n are not known.

– Insufficient

From statement 2:

We know that:

When the new group of students joins the class, the strength of the class increases by a number equal to the initial average age of the students in the class => $m = a$

Thus, from (i), we have:

$a(a - b - 1) = n$

However, the value of a cannot be determined since the values of b and n are not known.

– Insufficient

Thus, from both statements together:

From (i), we have:

$$a(a - 15 - 1) = n$$

$$=> a(a - 16) = n$$

However, the value of a cannot be determined since the value of n is not known. – Insufficient

The correct answer is option E.

79. The average of the first n positive integers, i.e. $1, 2, 3, \ldots n$ equals $\left(\dfrac{1+n}{2}\right)$, as the series is in Arithmetic Progression.

For example:

- $n = 5$: The average $= \dfrac{1+2+3+4+5}{5} = 3 = \dfrac{1+5}{2}$

  The average is an integer if n is odd

- $n = 6$: The average $= \dfrac{1+2+3+4+5+6}{6} = \dfrac{7}{2} = \dfrac{1+6}{2}$

  The average is not an integer if n is even

From statement 1:

We know that the average of the first $2n$ positive integers is not an integer.

This is obvious, since, $2n$ is an even integer (since it is given that n is an integer) and we have seen above that the average is not an integer if n is even.

Though $2n$ is even, the value of n may be either even or odd.

Hence, we cannot uniquely determine whether the average of the first n positive integers is an integer. – Insufficient

From statement 2:

We know that the average of the first $\dfrac{n}{2}$ positive integers is an integer.

Thus, we can definitely say that n must be even (else $\dfrac{n}{2}$ would have been a fraction and the above statement would not have any logical significance).

Thus, we get a specific answer, that the average of the first n positive integers is not an integer. – Sufficient

The correct answer is option B.

80. The average of the first n positive integers, i.e. $1, 2, 3, \ldots n$ equals $\left(\dfrac{1+n}{2}\right)$, as the series is in Arithmetic Progression.

The average of the first $(m + n)$ integers

$= \dfrac{1 + (m + n)}{2} \ldots \text{(i)}$

The average of the first $(m - n)$ integers

$= \dfrac{1 + (m - n)}{2} \ldots \text{(ii)}$

We need to determine whether the value of the expression in (i) is greater than thrice that in (ii), i.e. we have:

$\dfrac{1 + m + n}{2} > 3\left(\dfrac{1 + m - n}{2}\right)$

$\Rightarrow 1 + m + n > 3 + 3m - 3n$

$\Rightarrow 2n > m + 1 \ldots \text{(iii)}$

From statement 1:

We know that: $m > 2n$

$\Rightarrow m + 1 > 2n + 1$

However, from (iii), we observe that: $2n > m + 1$

$\Rightarrow 2n > m + 1 > 2n + 1$

$\Rightarrow 2n > 2n + 1$

The above is not possible since n is a positive integer.

Thus, the answer to the question is 'No'. – Sufficient

From statement 2:

We know that: $m < 3n$

We may have the following scenarios:

- $m = 5$, $n = 4$

  $\Rightarrow m < 3n$ and $2n > m + 1$ – The answer to the question is 'Yes'

- $m = 8$, $n = 4$

  $\Rightarrow m < 3n$ and $2n \not> m + 1$ – The answer to the question is 'No'

Thus, the answer cannot be uniquely determined. – Insufficient

The correct answer is option A.

81. Let the number of people in the group be n.

Let the average age of the members of the group be a.

Thus, sum of the ages of the members in the group = na years.

From statement 1:

We only know that:

$a < 22 \ldots$(i)

Thus, nothing can be inferred about the number of people in the group. – Insufficient

From statement 2:

If 3 people with average age 44 years leave the group, the number of members in the group decreases to $(n-3)$ and the total age decreases to $(na - 3 \times 44) = (na - 132)$ years.

Thus, the new average age of the members in the group

$= \left(\dfrac{na - 132}{n - 3}\right)$ years

Since the average age becomes half the initial value, we have: $\dfrac{na - 132}{n - 3} = \dfrac{a}{2}$

$=> 2na - 264 = na - 3a$

$=> a\,(n + 3) = 264 \ldots$(ii)

Since the value of a is not known, the number of people originally in the group may be 8, less than 8 or greater than 8. – Insufficient

Thus, from both statements together:

From (i): $a < 22$

Substituting the above in (ii):

$n + 3 > \dfrac{264}{22} => n + 3 > 11$

$=> n > 8$

Thus, the answer to the question is 'Yes'. – Sufficient

The correct answer is option C.

82. The average price of the mixture formed by mixing the two varieties of rice, a kg of one, priced at $\$x$ per kg and b kg of the other, priced at $\$(3x)$ per kg is

$$= \$\left(\frac{ax + 3bx}{a + b}\right) = \$x\left(\frac{a + 3b}{a + b}\right) \ldots (i)$$

From statement 1:

We have: $a > 2b$

We have to ensure whether:

$$x\left(\frac{a + 3b}{a + b}\right) > \frac{3}{2}x$$

$$=> \left(\frac{a + 3b}{a + b}\right) > \frac{3}{2} \text{ (Cancelling } x \text{ from both sides)}$$

$$=> 2a + 6b = 3a + 3b$$

$$=> 3b > a$$

For $a = 3$ & $b = 1$, $a > 2b$, but $3b \not> a$, answer is No.

However, for $a = 5$ & $b = 2$, $a > 2b$, and $3b > a$, answer is Yes.

Thus, the answer cannot be uniquely determined. – Insufficient

From statement 2:

We have: $a = 3b$

Thus, the average price, from (i)

$$= \$\left(\frac{3bx + 3bx}{3b + b}\right) = \$\left(\frac{3x}{2}\right)$$

Thus, the above price is not greater than $\$\left(\frac{3}{2}x\right)$.

The answer to the question is 'No'. – Sufficient

The correct answer is option B.

83. Let the smallest power of 2 be p and let there be k powers of 2 whose average is calculated.

Thus, the largest power of 2 is $(p + k - 1)$

Let us see how.

Say $p = 3$ & $k = 4$, thus the exponent numbers are: 2^3, 2^4, 2^5 & 2^6

We see that the largest exponent number 2^6 has a power of $6 = 3 + 4 - 1 = p + k - 1$

Thus, the required average

$$= \frac{2^p + 2^{p+1} + 2^{p+2} + \ldots 2^{p+k-1}}{k}$$

$$= 2^p \times \left(\frac{1 + 2 + 2^2 + \cdots + 2^{k-1}}{k} \right)$$

From statement 1:

We have: $p = 7$

However, the value of k is unknown. – Insufficient

From statement 2:

We have: $k = 4$

Thus, the required average

$$= 2^p \times \left(\frac{1 + 2 + 2^2 + 2^3}{4} \right) = 2^p \times \left(\frac{15}{4} \right)$$

However, the value of p is unknown.

Thus, the above may or may not be an integer, depending on the value of p. – Insufficient

Thus, from both statements together:

The required average

$$= 2^7 \times \left(\frac{15}{4} \right) = 2^5 \times 15$$

Thus, the above is an integer. – Sufficient

Note: The following is an interesting property, though we don't need to use this to solve the above problem:

The average of n consecutive powers of 2, starting from 2^0, i.e. $\left(\frac{2^0 + 2^1 + 2^2 + \cdots + 2^{n-1}}{n} \right)$ is never an integer for $n > 1$

The correct answer is option C.

84. From statement 1:

The average salary of an engineer and the average salary of a supervisor are unknowns.

We only know that the average salary of all engineers and supervisors is $50 and that of 40% of the engineers and 60% of the supervisors is $45.

Thus, we can only conclude that since the proportional share of engineers is reduced as compared to supervisors and as a result, the average salary gets reduced, engineers must earn more than supervisors.

We cannot comment on the number of engineers and the number of supervisors. – Insufficient

From statement 2:

Statement 2 is similar to Statement 1. Hence, the same reasoning follows. – Insufficient

Thus, from both statements together:

We can see that:

For 100% engineers and 100% supervisors, the average salary is $50.

For 40% engineers and 60% supervisors, the average salary is $45, i.e. there is a decrease of $5.

For 60% engineers and 40% supervisors, the average salary is $55, i.e. there is an increase of $5.

Thus, we see that the increase and decrease in the average is of the same value when the percentages of engineers and supervisors are interchanged.

Thus, the effect on the average is the same, only of different sign, implying that the number of engineers and the number of supervisors must have been same, with engineers having a higher salary than the supervisors.

The correct answer is option C.

85. Let the temperatures on Monday, Tuesday, Wednesday, Thursday, and Friday be denoted by m, t, w, r and f, respectively.

From statement 1:

Since the average temperature on Monday, Tuesday, Wednesday and Thursday was 30°
C, we have:

$$\frac{m + t + w + r}{4} = 30$$

$$=> m + t + w + r = 120 \ldots(i)$$

The value of m cannot be determined from (i) alone. – Insufficient

From statement 2:

Since the average for Tuesday, Wednesday, Thursday and Friday was 25° C, we have:
$$\frac{t + w + r + f}{4} = 25$$

$$=> t + w + r + f = 100 \ldots(ii)$$

Since there is no information about m, its value cannot be determined. – Insufficient

Thus, from both statements together:

Subtracting (ii) from (i):

$$m - f = 20 \ldots(iii)$$

The value of m cannot be determined from the above equation. – Insufficient

The correct answer is option E.

86. Let Dan's average mark after the first 4 tests be x.

   From statement 1:

   There is no information about the first four tests. – Insufficient

   From statement 2:

   We only know that the difference between Dan's average mark after the first four tests
   and the average mark after the first five tests is an integer.

   The value of the average mark for the first 4 tests cannot be determined only using the
   above information. – Insufficient

   Thus, from both statements together:

Total marks in the first 4 tests = $4x$

Since Dan scored 88 in the fifth test, the total after 5 tests = $4x + 88$

Thus, average mark in 5 tests = $\dfrac{4x + 88}{5}$

Thus, increase in average mark = $\dfrac{4x + 88}{5} - x = \dfrac{88 - x}{5}$

Since the increase is an integer, $(88 - x)$ is divisible by 5.

Thus, possible values of x could be: 3, 8, 13, 18, 23 … 83, 88

Thus, the value of x cannot be uniquely determined. – Insufficient

The correct answer is option E.

87. Let us assume that A and B meet at 12:00 noon at X.

Since A was late by t minutes, we need to find the time when A would reach X. The difference between this time and 12:00 noon would give us the value of t.

From statement 1:

We have no information about the position of the new meeting point, Y, with respect to the earlier meeting point, X. – Insufficient

From statement 2:

We have no information about the speeds of A and B. – Insufficient

Thus, from both statements together:

We know that Y is 1.2 km away from X (Y is nearer to A than X since A was late).

Since B was on time, he must have reached X at 12:00 noon (actual meeting time).

Time taken by B to travel 1.2 km to reach Y = $\dfrac{1.2}{12}$ = 0.1 hours = 6 minutes.

Thus, B reaches Y at 12:06 pm.

Since A and B meet at Y, A was also at Y at 12:06 pm.

Time taken by A to cover 1.2 km to reach X = $\dfrac{1.2}{6}$ = 0.2 hours = 12 minutes.

Thus, A reaches X at 12:06 + 12 min. = 12:18 pm.

Thus, we observe that A reaches X 18 minutes later that when he was supposed to reach.

Thus, we have: $t = 18$ – Sufficient

The correct answer is option C.

88. Let the distance the man covers upstream be d miles.

Let the speed of the slower boat in still water be b miles per hour.

Let the speed of the stream be r miles per hour.

Thus, speed while going upstream = $(b - r)$ miles per hour.

Thus, time taken to cover d miles upstream = $\left(\dfrac{d}{b - r}\right)$ hours.

Thus, we have:

$$\frac{d}{b - r} = 6 \dots \text{(i)}$$

If the man uses a boat that is twice as fast in still water as the earlier one, the speed of the faster boat in still water = $2b$ miles per hour.

Thus, upstream speed = $(2b - r)$ miles per hour.

Thus, time taken to cover d miles upstream = $\left(\dfrac{d}{2b - r}\right)$ hours.

Thus, we need to determine the value of $\left(\dfrac{d}{2b - r}\right)$.

From statement 1:

Speed while going downstream using the slower boat = $(b + r)$ miles per hour.

Thus, time taken to cover d miles downstream = $\left(\dfrac{d}{b + r}\right)$ hours.

Thus, we have:

$$\frac{d}{b + r} = 4 \dots \text{(ii)}$$

Dividing (i) by (ii):

$$\frac{b + r}{b - r} = \frac{6}{4} => 4b + 4r = 6b - 6r$$

$$=> b = 5r$$

Thus, from (ii):

$$\frac{d}{5r + r} = 4 => d = 24r$$

Thus, we have:

$$\frac{d}{2b - r} = \frac{24r}{10r - r} = \frac{8}{3} \text{ - Sufficient}$$

From statement 2:

Only knowing the actual value of the distance does not help to establish a relation between b and r. – Insufficient

The correct answer is option A.

89. We know that average speed is the ratio of total distance to total time.

From statement 1:

There is no information about the speeds. – Insufficient

From statement 2:

There is no information about the distances or the ratio of the distances. – Insufficient

Thus, from both statements together:

Apparently, it seems that, since it is not specified that which distance was covered at a particular speed, the answer cannot be determined.

However, the question asks whether the average speed CAN exceed 23 miles per hour.

The average speed would be maximized if the man travels the larger distance at the higher speed.

Thus, let us assume that the distances are $4x$ miles and $5x$ miles and the man travels $5x$ miles at 30 miles per hour and $4x$ miles at 16 miles per hour.

Thus, the total time taken = $\left(\frac{4x}{16} + \frac{5x}{30} \right) = \frac{5x}{12}$ hours

Also, total distance = $4x + 5x = 9x$ miles

Thus, average speed

$$= \frac{9x}{\left(\frac{5x}{12} \right)} = \frac{108}{5}$$

$= 21.6$ miles per hour

Since the maximum average speed is less than 23 miles per hour, the answer to the question is 'No'. – Sufficient

The correct answer is option C.

90. Let the distance between P and Q be x meters.

Let the speeds of A and B be a meters per second and b meters per second, respectively. We need to determine the value of $\left(\frac{a}{b}\right)$.

From statement 1:

While traveling in opposite directions, they meet 300 meters from Q.

Thus, distance travelled by B = 300 meter

Distance travelled by A = $(x - 300)$ meter

Since ratio of the distances travelled by A and B equals the ratio of the speeds of A and B, we have:

$$\frac{a}{b} = \frac{x - 300}{300} \ldots \text{(i)}$$

However, since x is unknown, the value of $\left(\frac{a}{b}\right)$ cannot be determined. – Insufficient

From statement 2:

While traveling in the same direction, they meet 400 meters from Q.

Thus, distance travelled by B = 400 meter

Distance travelled by A = $(x + 400)$ meter

Since ratio of the distances travelled by A and B equals the ratio of the speeds of A and B, we have:

$$\frac{a}{b} = \frac{x + 400}{400} \ldots \text{(ii)}$$

However, since x is unknown, the value of $\left(\frac{a}{b}\right)$ cannot be determined. – Insufficient

Thus, from both statements together:

Equating (i) and (ii):

$$\frac{x - 300}{300} = \frac{x + 400}{400}$$

$$=> 4x - 1200 = 3x + 1200$$

$$=> x = 2400$$

$$\Rightarrow \frac{a}{b} = \frac{x + 400}{400} = \frac{2800}{400} = \frac{7}{1} \text{ - Sufficient}$$

The correct answer is option C.

91. Average speed is calculated as the ratio of the total distance travelled to the total time taken.

Total distance = $(x + y)$ miles

Total time = $\left(\dfrac{x}{p} + \dfrac{y}{q} \right)$ hours

Thus, average speed = $\dfrac{x + y}{\left(\dfrac{x}{p} + \dfrac{y}{q} \right)}$

$= \dfrac{pq\,(x + y)}{py + qx} \dots \text{(i)}$

We need to determine whether:

$$\frac{pq\,(x + y)}{py + qx} = \frac{p + q}{2}$$

From statement 1:

Substituting $x = y$ in (i):

Average speed

$= \dfrac{pq\,(x + y)}{py + qx} = \dfrac{pq \times 2x}{px + qx} = \dfrac{2pq}{p + q} \neq \left(\dfrac{p + q}{2} \right)$

The answer to the question is 'No'.

From statement 2:

Substituting $2py = qx$ in (i):

Average speed

$= \dfrac{pq\,(x + y)}{py + qx} = \dfrac{pqx + pqy}{py + qx} = \dfrac{p\,(qx) + q\,(py)}{py + qx} = \dfrac{p\,(2py) + q\,(py)}{py + 2py}$

$= \dfrac{py\,(2p + q)}{3py} = \dfrac{2p + q}{3} \neq \left(\dfrac{p + q}{2} \right)$

The answer to the question is 'No'.

The correct answer is option D.

92. Let the distance from home to school be $2d$.

Let the speed of walking, cycling and riding the cab be w, c and b, respectively.

Time taken to cycle = $\dfrac{2d}{c}$

Time taken to walk over distance d and ride a cab over distance d = $\left(\dfrac{d}{w} + \dfrac{d}{b} \right)$

We need to determine whether:

$\dfrac{d}{w} + \dfrac{d}{b} \le \dfrac{2d}{c}$

From statement 1:

There is no information about the speed of the cab. – Insufficient

From statement 2:

There is no information about his walking speed. – Insufficient

Thus, from both statements together:

We have: $b = 3c$ and $c = 3w$

$=> b = 9w$

Thus, we have:

Time taken to cycle

$= \dfrac{2d}{c} = \dfrac{2}{3} \left(\dfrac{d}{w} \right)$

Time taken to cycle over distance d and ride a cab over distance d

$= \dfrac{d}{w} + \dfrac{d}{b} = \dfrac{d}{w} + \dfrac{d}{9w}$

$= \dfrac{10}{9} \left(\dfrac{d}{w} \right) > \dfrac{2}{3} \left(\dfrac{d}{w} \right)$

Thus, the boy takes longer if he walks and takes a cab than if he cycled.

The answer to the question is 'No'. – Sufficient

The correct answer is option C.

93. From statement 1:

Since A covers 5 laps in the same time when B covers 4 laps, we have:

Ratio of speeds of A and B equals the ratio of their distances = 5 : 4 … (i)

However, there is no information about C. – Insufficient

From statement 2:

Since B and C run in opposite directions and B covers 400 meters for the first meeting, distance covered by C = 1200 – 400 = 800 meters.

Thus, we have:

Ratio of speeds of B and C equals the ratio of their distances = 400 : 800 = 4 : 8 … (ii)

However, there is no information about A. – Insufficient

Thus, from both statements together:

Combining (i) and (ii):

Ratio of speeds of A and C = 5 : 8 – Sufficient

The correct answer is option C.

94. Let the total distance be $2d$ miles.

Time taken to cover d miles at 20 miles per hour = $\dfrac{d}{20}$ hours.

From statement 1:

Time taken to cover the remaining d miles at 40 miles per hour = $\dfrac{d}{40}$ hours.

However, there is no information regarding the actual time taken. – Insufficient

From statement 2:

We know that if the boy travelled the remaining distance at 30 miles per hour, he would reach his destination 15 minutes or $\dfrac{1}{4}$ hours late.

Time taken to cover the remaining d miles at 30 miles per hour = $\dfrac{d}{30}$ hours.

However, there is no information regarding the actual time taken. – Insufficient

Thus, from both statements together:

$\dfrac{d}{30} - \dfrac{d}{40} = \dfrac{1}{4}$

$=> d = 30$

Thus, total distance = $2d$ = 60 miles. – Sufficient

The correct answer is option C.

95. From statement 1:

We know that the ratio of speeds of A and B is 5 : 3

Thus, for the meeting between A and B, since B covered 300 meters, A must have covered $\frac{5}{3} \times 300 = 500$ meters

Thus, when A and B return towards P, A would have to cover 500 meters.

Since the speed ratios of A and B is 5 : 3, in the time that A covered 500 meters, B would only be able to cover $\frac{3}{5} \times 500 = 300$ meters.

Thus, B would be 200 meters behind A. – Sufficient

From statement 2:

We know that the total distance between the points P and Q is 800 meters.

Thus, for the meeting between A and B, since B covered 300 meters, A must have covered 800 – 300 = 500 meters.

This is the same scenario as discussed under the first statement. – Sufficient

The correct answer is option D.

96. Let the time John takes to walk from his home to school be w minutes.

Let the time John takes to run from his home to school be r minutes.

From statement 1:

$r + w = 40 \ldots$ (i)

Since the individual values of r and w are not known, the answer cannot be determined. – Insufficient

From statement 2:

$r + r = 30$

$\Rightarrow r = 15 \ldots$ (ii)

However, there is no information about w. – Insufficient

Thus, from both statements together:

Using (i) and (ii):

$w = 40 - 15 = 25 \ldots (\text{iii})$

Thus, ratio of John's running and walking speeds is inverse of the times taken while running and walking, respectively (since the distance is constant)

$= 25 : 15 = 5 : 3$

Thus, the required percent

$= \dfrac{5 - 3}{3} \times 100 = 66.7\% - \text{Sufficient}$

The correct answer is option C.

97.   We know that:

A and B can complete the work in 20 days, while B and C can complete the work in 25 days.

From statement 1:

We know that:

A works for the first 4 days alone, then B works the next 9 days alone and finally C works for 23 days alone to complete the work.

Thus, we have:

Total work

= A's 4 days' work + B's 9 days' work + C's 23 days' work

= A's 4 days' work + B's 9 or (4 + 5) days' work + C's 23 or (5 + 18) days' work

= (A's 4 days' work + B's 4 days' work) + (B's 5 days' work + C's 5 days' work) + C's 18 days' work

= (A + B)'s 4 days' work + (B + C)'s 5 days' work + C's 18 days' work

Part of the work done by A and B in 4 days = $\dfrac{4}{20} = \dfrac{1}{5}$

Part of the work done by B and C in 5 days $= \dfrac{5}{25} = \dfrac{1}{5}$

Thus, part of the work done by C is 18 days $= \left(1 - \dfrac{1}{5} - \dfrac{1}{5}\right) = \dfrac{3}{5}$

Thus, time taken by C to complete the entire work $= \dfrac{18}{\left(\dfrac{3}{5}\right)} = 18 \times \dfrac{5}{3} = 30$ days. – Sufficient

From statement 2:

We know that: B can complete the entire work in 150 days

Thus, part of the work completed by B in 1 day $= \dfrac{1}{150}$

Since B and C can complete the work in 25 days, i.e. work done per day is $\dfrac{1}{25}$, we have:

Part of the work completed by C in 1 day $= \dfrac{1}{25} - \dfrac{1}{150} = \dfrac{1}{30}$

Thus, time taken by C to complete the entire work $= \dfrac{1}{\left(\dfrac{1}{30}\right)} = 30$ days. – Sufficient

The correct answer is option D.

98.   We know that:

A, B and C start working together on a project with C leaving after $\dfrac{1}{4}$ of the project was completed and B leaving after another $\dfrac{1}{4}$ of the project was completed.

Thus, A, B and C worked together for $\dfrac{1}{4}$ of the project, A and B worked for another $\dfrac{1}{4}$ of the project and finally, A worked alone for the remaining $\left(1 - \dfrac{1}{4} - \dfrac{1}{4}\right) = \dfrac{1}{2}$ of the project.

From statement 1:

We know that A and B can complete the project in 20 and 30 days, respectively.

Thus, part of the work done by A and B together in 1 day $= \dfrac{1}{20} + \dfrac{1}{30} = \dfrac{1}{12}$

Thus, time taken by A and B to complete the project together = 12 days.

Thus, the time taken by A and B to complete $\dfrac{1}{4}$ of the project $= \dfrac{12}{4} = 3$ days.

Since A, B and C were working on the first $\dfrac{1}{4}$ of the project, the time taken would be less than 3 days . . . (i)

Again, for the next $\dfrac{1}{4}$ of the project, only A and B were working.

Thus, time taken = 3 days . . . (ii)

For the last half of the project, only A was working.

Thus, time taken by A = $\frac{20}{2}$ = 10 days ... (iii)

Thus, from (i) (ii) and (iii), we have:

Total time for the entire project is greater than 13 days, but less than 16 days. Ideally, the value of (i) cannot be 3 as no matter how slow worker C may be, value of (i) cannot reach '3'.

Thus, the answer to the question is 'Yes'. – Sufficient

From statement 2:

There is no information about the time taken by A and B. – Insufficient

The correct answer is option A.

99. We know that:

Time taken by C = 2 × Time taken by A and B together for the same work

Since rate of doing work and time taken to complete a work are inversely proportional, we have:

=> Work done by C = $\frac{1}{2}$ × Work done by A and B together in the same time

=> Work done by A and B together in the same time = 2 × Work done by C

Adding 'Work done by C' to both sides:

=> Work done by A, B and C together = 3 × Work done by C in the same time ... (i)

=> Time taken by A, B and C together = $\frac{1}{3}$ × Time taken by C for the same work ... (ii)

From statement 1:

There is no information about the actual time taken by A, B or C. – Insufficient

From statement 2:

There is no information about the actual time taken by A or C. – Insufficient

Thus, from both statements together:

From Statement 1, we know that:

A takes twice as long to complete a work as C

=> Time taken by A = 2 × Time taken by C for the same work

=> Work done by A = $\frac{1}{2}$ × Work done by C in the same time

=> Work done by C = 2 × Work done by A in the same time ... (iii)

Thus, from (i) and (iii), we have, in the same time:

Work done by A, B and C together = 3 × Work done by C = 6 × Work done by A

Thus, we have:

Work done by C = $\frac{1}{3}$ × Work done by A, B and C together in the same time

Work done by A = $\frac{1}{6}$ × Work done by A, B and C together in the same time

Thus, we have:

Work done by B = $\left(1 - \frac{1}{3} - \frac{1}{6}\right)$ × Work done by A, B and C together in the same time

=> Work done by B = $\frac{1}{2}$ × Work done by A, B and C together in the same time

=> Time taken by B alone = 2 × Time taken by A, B and C together for the same work

Thus, from Statement 2:

=> Time taken by A, B and C together = $\frac{1}{2}$× × 20 = 10 days. – Sufficient

The correct answer is option C.

100. From statement 1:

There is no information about the machines Q and R.

From statement 2:

There is no information about machine P.

Thus, from both statements together:

Number of units of item A manufactured in 9 hours @ 5 units in every three hours $= \frac{5}{3} \times 9 = 15$

Since machine Q is 20% faster, it can manufacture 20% more units of item B than the number of units of item A manufactured by machine P.

Thus, number of units of item B manufactured in 9 hours = 120% of 15 $= \dfrac{120}{100} \times 15 = 18$

Since machine Q is 20% slower, it can manufacture 20% fewer units of item C than the number of units of item A manufactured by machine P.

Thus, number of units of item C manufactured in 9 hours = 80% of 15 $= \dfrac{80}{100} \times 15 = 12$

We know that three units of A, two units of B and one unit of C are required to manufacture the final product.

Thus, we have:

- Number of such groups of 3 units of A $= \dfrac{15}{3} = 5$
- Number of such groups of 2 units of B $= \dfrac{18}{2} = 9$
- Number of units of C = 12

Thus, the number of units of the final product

= The least among 5, 9 and 12 = 5 – Sufficient

The correct answer is option C.

101. We know that:

Filling rate of pipe A = 12 liters per minute

Filling rate of pipe B = 15 liters per minute

From statement 1:

Time taken by pipes A and C to fill a tank twice as large = 30 minutes

Thus, time taken by pipes A and C to fill the given tank $= \dfrac{30}{2} = 15$ minutes

However, there is no information about the time taken by pipe B to fill the tank. Also, there is no information about the capacity of the tank. – Insufficient

From statement 2:

Time taken by pipe C to fill the given tank = 45 minutes

There is no information about the time taken by pipes A or B to fill the tank. – Insufficient

Thus, from both statements together:

We know that the time taken by pipes A and C to fill the given tank is 15 minutes

=> Part of the tank filled by A and C in 1 minute = $\dfrac{1}{15}$

Also, time taken by pipe C to fill the given tank is 45 minutes

=> Part of the tank filled by C in 1 minute = $\dfrac{1}{45}$

=> Part of the tank filled by A in 1 minute = $\dfrac{1}{15} - \dfrac{1}{45} = \dfrac{2}{45}$

=> Time taken by A to fill the tank = $\dfrac{45}{2}$ minutes

=> Capacity of the tank = $\dfrac{45}{2} \times 12 = 270$ liters

=> Filling rate of pipe C = $\dfrac{270}{45} = 6$ liters per minute

Thus, for all three pipes together, total filling rate = 12 + 15 + 6 = 33 liters per minute

=> Time taken by all three pipes together to fill the tank = $\dfrac{270}{33}$ minutes. – Sufficient

The correct answer is option C.

102. We know that A and B can complete a work in 40 days ... (i)

From statement 1:

B and C can complete the work in 30 days ... (ii)

Thus, from (i) and (ii), we see that if A is replaced by C, the time required for the work decreases.

Thus, the efficiency of C must be greater than that of A.

Thus, the efficiency of A cannot be the greatest among A, B and C. – Sufficient

From statement 2:

We only know that the time taken by C to complete the work is 50 days.

Since the individual times taken by A and B are not known, the efficiency of A cannot be compared with that of B or C. – Insufficient

The correct answer is option A.

103. From statement 1:

There is no information about the working efficiency of women.

From statement 2:

We have:

Area painted by 2 men in 1 hour is the same as that painted by 1 woman in 2 hours.

Thus, the efficiencies of men and women are the same.

Thus, we have:

To paint 20 square feet, 2 men take 1 hour

Thus, to paint (60×80) or 2400 square feet, time taken by 2 men = $\frac{1}{20} \times 2400 = 120$ hours

Thus, to pain 2400 square feet, time taken by $(4 + 6)$ or 10 men = $120 \times \frac{2}{10} = 24$ hours – Sufficient

The correct answer is option B.

104. Let the time taken by B be x hours.

Thus, time taken by A = $(t - x)$ hours.

From statement 1:

We only know that x and $(t - x)$ are positive integers.

Since there is no other information, we cannot determine whether $t > 20$ – Insufficient

From statement 2:

Time taken by A and B together = 3 hours.

Note: The sum of the times taken by A and B individually is NOT the time taken by A and B to complete the work together.

Part of work done by A and B, working alone, in 1 hour = $\left(\frac{1}{t - x}\right)$ and $\left(\frac{1}{x}\right)$, respectively

Also, part of work done by A and B together in 1 hour = $\frac{1}{3}$

Thus, we have:

$$\frac{1}{t-x} + \frac{1}{x} = \frac{1}{3}$$

$$=> \frac{x+t-x}{(t-x)\,x} = \frac{1}{3}$$

$$=> 3t = tx - x^2 => t\,(x-3) = x^2$$

$$=> t = \frac{x^2}{x-3} \ldots (i)$$

The value of t can be different for different values of x.

For example:

- $x = 4$: $t = \dfrac{4^2}{1} = 16 \not> 20$ – The answer to the question is 'No'

- $x = 3.5$: $t = \dfrac{3.5^2}{0.5} = 2 \times \left(\dfrac{7}{2}\right)^2 = 24.5 > 20$ – The answer to the question is 'Yes'

Thus, the answer cannot be uniquely determined. – Insufficient

Thus, from both statements together:

We know that x and t are positive integers.

Thus, from (i), we have:

$(x-3)$ must be a factor of x^2

Thus, rearranging terms, we have:

$$t = \frac{(x^2 - 9) + 9}{x - 3}$$

$$=> t = \frac{x^2 - 9}{x-3} + \frac{9}{x-3}$$

$$=> t = x + 3 + \frac{9}{x-3}$$

Since t and $(x+3)$ are integers, $(x-3)$ must be a factor of 9

Thus, we have:

- $x - 3 = 1 => x = 4 => t = 16$

- $x - 3 = 3 => x = 6 => t = 12$

- $x - 3 = 9 => x = 12 => t = 16$

Thus, we have: $t \not> 20$.

The answer to the question is 'No'. – Sufficient

The correct answer is option C.

105. From statement 1:

We know that:

To complete a work in 15 days, number of workers employed = 20

Thus, to complete the work in 10 days, number of workers required = $\dfrac{20 \times 15}{10} = 30$

Thus, additional number of workers required = 30 – 20 = 10

However, this is true only if the additional workers had been employed in the very beginning.

Since already x days ($x \neq 0$) work was done with only 20 workers, to finish the work inside 10 days, one would require more than 10 additional workers.

Thus, the work cannot be completed inside 10 days.

Thus, the answer to the question is 'No'. – Sufficient

From statement 2:

The value of x alone is not sufficient to answer the question.

The number of additional workers employed, i.e. n must also be known to get a definite answer. – Insufficient

The correct answer is option A.

106. From statement 1:

Let John takes x steps per minute.

Since the number of steps he takes per minute is 25 times his speed measured in meters per second, we have:

John's speed = $\left(\dfrac{x}{25}\right)$ meters per second.

Thus, distance John covers in one second = $\left(\dfrac{x}{25}\right)$ meters.

Number of steps John takes in one second = $\left(\dfrac{x}{60}\right)$.

Thus, we can say that in $\left(\dfrac{x}{60}\right)$ steps, John covers $\left(\dfrac{x}{25}\right)$ meters.

Thus, in one step, distance covered by John

$$= \frac{\left(\dfrac{x}{25}\right)}{\left(\dfrac{x}{60}\right)} = \frac{60}{25}$$

$$= \frac{12}{5} \text{ meters. – Sufficient}$$

From statement 2:

We only know that John runs at a speed of 5 meters per second.

There is no information about the number of steps he takes. – Insufficient

The correct answer is option A.

107. Let x pounds of the costlier variety and y pounds of the cheaper variety be mixed.

Let the price of the cheaper variety be $\$c$ per pound.

Thus, the price of the costlier variety is $\$(c + 15)$ per pound.

Thus, the average price of the mixture per pound (weighted average) = $\$\left(\dfrac{cx + (c + 15)\,y}{x + y}\right)$

From statement 1:

Since the average price of the mixture is $20 per pound, we have: $\dfrac{cx + (c + 15)\,y}{x + y} = 20$

Since the value of c is unknown, we cannot determine the ratio of $x : y$ – Insufficient

From statement 2:

Since the average price of the mixture is $7 per pound cheaper than the costlier variety, we have:

$$\frac{cx + (c + 15)\,y}{x + y} = (c + 15) - 7$$

$$=> cx + cy + 15y = (x + y)(c + 8)$$

$$=> cx + cy + 15y = cx + cy + 8x + 8y$$

$$=> 8x = 7y$$

$$=> x : y = 7 : 8 \text{ – Sufficient}$$

The correct answer is option B.

108. Let the distances the man covered at 20 miles per hour and 30 miles per hour be x miles and y miles, respectively.

Thus, time taken to cover x miles = $\left(\dfrac{x}{20}\right)$ hours … (i)

Time taken to cover y miles = $\left(\dfrac{y}{30}\right)$ hours … (ii)

From statement 1:

Since average speed is the ratio of total distance to total time, and is given as 24 miles per hour, we have:

$$\frac{x+y}{\left(\dfrac{x}{20}+\dfrac{y}{30}\right)} = 24$$

$$=> x + y = \frac{24x}{20} + \frac{24y}{30}$$

$$=> \frac{4x}{20} = \frac{6y}{30}$$

$$=> x = y \dots \text{(iii)}$$

However, the numerical value of x or y cannot be determined. – Insufficient

From statement 2:

We know that the ratio of the time for which he travelled at 20 miles per hour and that for which he travelled at 30 miles per hour is 3 : 2.

Thus, from (i) and (ii):

$$\frac{x}{20} : \frac{y}{30} = 3 : 2$$

$$=> x = y \dots \text{(iv)}$$

However, the numerical value of x or y cannot be determined. – Insufficient

Thus, from both statements together:

Even after combining both statements, the numerical value of x or y cannot be determined. – Insufficient

The correct answer is option E.

109. From statement 1:

There is no information about the ratio of the speeds of A and B. – Insufficient

From statement 2:

There is no information about the exact times when A and B start their respective journeys. – Insufficient

Thus, from both statements together:

We know that the ratio of the times taken by A and B to cover the same distance

= 9 : 6 = 3 : 2

Thus, ratio of the speeds of A and B is the inverse of the ratio of their speeds as the distance is constant.

= 2 : 3

Thus, let us assume the speeds of A and B to be $2x$ miles per hour and $3x$ miles per hour.

Thus, the distance between the points P and Q = $9 \times 2x = 18x$ miles or $6 \times 3x = 18x$ miles.

Since A started 2 hours before B, the distance covered by A from 9:00 am to 11:00 am = $2 \times 2x = 4x$ miles.

Thus, remaining distance = $18x - 4x = 14x$ miles.

At 11:00 am, both A and B are traveling towards each other.

Thus, their relative speed as they are traveling in opposite direction = $2x + 3x = 5x$ miles per hour.

Thus, time taken to meet

$= \dfrac{14x}{5x} = 2.8$ hours = 2 hours 48 minutes

Thus, the meeting time is 2 hours 48 minutes past 11:00 am, i.e. 1:48 pm. – Sufficient

The correct answer is option C.

110.   From statement 1:

There is no information about the length of the steps taken by A and B. – Insufficient

From statement 2:

There is no information about the time taken by A and B to take their strides. – Insufficient

Thus, from both statements together:

We know that:

3 steps of A are of the same length of 5 steps of B

$=>$ 1 step of A $= \dfrac{5}{3}$ steps of B ... (i)

We also know that:

For every 5 steps taken by A, B takes 8 steps

$=>$ Time taken by A to take 5 steps = Time taken by B to take 8 steps

$=>$ Time taken by A to take 1 step = Time taken by B to take $\dfrac{8}{5}$ steps ... (ii)

Thus, from (i) and (ii):

Time taken by A to cover a length of $\dfrac{5}{3}$ steps of B = Time taken by B to take $\dfrac{8}{5}$ steps

$=>$ Time taken by A to cover a length of 1 step of B = Time taken by B to take $\dfrac{8}{5} \times \dfrac{3}{5}$ steps

$=>$ Time taken by A to cover a length of 1 step of B = Time taken by B to take $\dfrac{24}{25}$ steps

$=>$ Time taken by A to cover a length of 1 step of B = $\dfrac{24}{25} \times$ Time taken by B to take 1 step

Thus, to cover the same distance (equal to 1 step of B), time taken by A is $\dfrac{24}{25}$ times the time taken by B

$=>$ A takes lesser time than B to cover the same distance

Thus, A would win the contest.

The answer to the question is 'Yes'. – Sufficient

The correct answer is option C.

Alternate approach:

Let us assume that: 3 steps of A = 5 steps of B = 15 meters

$=>$ 1 step of A = 5 meters and 1 step of B = 3 meters

=> 5 steps of A = 25 meters and 8 steps of B = 24 meters

Thus, when A covers 25 meters, B covers 24 meters => A is faster than B

Thus, A would win the contest.

111. From statement 1:

There is no information about the number of trips made by the boy. – Insufficient

From statement 2:

There is no information about the actual speeds with which the boy makes the trips. – Insufficient

Thus, from both statements together:

Since the maximum speed of the boy is 16 meters per second, the speeds are:

- 2 meters per second (first leg)

- 4 meters per second (return leg)

- 8 meters per second (second leg)

- 16 meters per second (second return leg)

Let the distance between the points P and Q be d meters.

Thus, the total time taken = $\dfrac{d}{2} + \dfrac{d}{4} + \dfrac{d}{8} + \dfrac{d}{16} = \dfrac{15d}{16}$ seconds.

Also, total distance travelled = $4d$ meters.

Thus, average speed = $\dfrac{4d}{\left(\dfrac{15d}{16}\right)} = \dfrac{64}{15}$ meters per second. – Sufficient

The correct answer is option C.

112. Let the distances covered by train and by bus be x miles and y miles, respectively.

We are expected to find $x : y$

From statement 1:

Time taken by train = $\left(\dfrac{x}{80}\right)$ hours.

Time taken by bus = $\left(\dfrac{y}{60}\right)$ hours.

Thus, the total time taken = $\left(\dfrac{x}{80} + \dfrac{y}{60}\right)$ hours ... (i)

However, there is no information about the distances travelled or about the total time. – Insufficient

From statement 2:

Time taken if he travelled only by train = $\left(\dfrac{x+y}{80}\right)$ hours.

Since this is $\dfrac{4}{5}$ of the actual time, we have:

Actual time taken = $\dfrac{5}{4}\left(\dfrac{x+y}{80}\right)$ hours ... (ii)

However, there is no information about the distances travelled or about the total time. – Insufficient

Thus, from both statements together:

From (i) and (ii), we have:

$\dfrac{x}{80} + \dfrac{y}{60} = \dfrac{5}{4}\left(\dfrac{x+y}{80}\right)$

$=> \dfrac{3x+4y}{240} = \dfrac{5x+5y}{320}$

$=> 12x + 16y = 15x + 15y$

$=> \dfrac{x}{y} = \dfrac{1}{3}$ – Sufficient

The correct answer is option C.

113.   From statement 1:

Since the cycling speed is thrice of the walking speed, the time taken to reach school by cycling will be $\dfrac{1}{3}$ of the time taken while walking (since the distance is the same, time taken varies inversely with the speed).

Thus, if the boy normally takes t minutes to reach school while walking, he would take $\dfrac{t}{3}$ minutes while cycling ... (i)

Thus, time saved = $t - \dfrac{t}{3} = \dfrac{2t}{3}$ minutes.

Thus, he would reach $\dfrac{2t}{3}$ minutes early ... (ii)

However, the actual time t taken while walking is not known. – Insufficient

From statement 2:

Since the speed of the car is twice the cycling speed, the time taken to reach school by car will be $\frac{1}{2}$ of the time taken while cycling.

Thus, if the boy normally takes T minutes to reach school while cycling, he would take $\frac{T}{2}$ minutes by car.

Thus, time saved $= T - \frac{T}{2} = \frac{T}{2}$ minutes.

Thus, he would reach $\frac{T}{2}$ minutes early.

Thus, we have: $\frac{T}{2} = 10 => T = 20$ minutes

Thus, the boy takes 20 minutes while cycling … (iii)

However, we have no information about the time he takes while walking. – Insufficient

Thus, from both statements together:

From (i) and (iii):

$\frac{t}{3} = 20 => t = 60$ minutes

Thus, from (ii), we have:

$\frac{2t}{3} = \frac{2}{3} \times 60 = 40$ minutes – Sufficient

The correct answer is option C.

114.   Let the distance between the homes of A and B be d km.

Let the speeds of A and B be a miles per hour and b miles per hour, respectively.

Thus, ratio of the distances covered by A and B would be the ratio of their speeds, i.e. $a : b$.

Thus, distance travelled by A $= \left(\dfrac{a}{a + b} \right) \times d$ miles … (i)

Distance travelled by B $= \left(\dfrac{b}{a + b} \right) \times d$ miles … (ii)

If the speed of B is 20% higher, i.e. $\left(\dfrac{120}{100} \times b \right) = \dfrac{6b}{5}$ miles per hour, we have:

Ratio of the distances covered by A and B $= a : \dfrac{6b}{5} = 5a : 6b$.

Thus, distance travelled by A $= \left(\dfrac{5a}{5a + 6b} \right) \times d$ miles … (iii)

Distance travelled by B = $\left(\dfrac{6b}{5a + 6b}\right) \times d$ miles ... (iv)

From statement 1:

We have:

$a = 9$ and $b = 15$

However, using this alone, the value of d cannot be determined. – Insufficient

From statement 2:

There is no information about the speeds of A and B. – Insufficient

Thus, from both statements together:

From (i), we have:

Distance travelled by A = $\left(\dfrac{9}{9 + 15}\right) \times d = \dfrac{3d}{8}$ miles

From (iii), we have:

Distance travelled by A when B travels at higher speed = $\left(\dfrac{5 \times 9}{5 \times 9 + 6 \times 15}\right) \times d = \dfrac{d}{3}$ miles

Thus, the difference between the distances covered by A = $\left(\dfrac{3d}{8} - \dfrac{d}{3}\right) = \dfrac{d}{24}$ miles

Since the distance between the two meeting points P and Q is 2 miles, we have:

$\dfrac{d}{24} = 2 \Rightarrow d = 48$ miles. – Sufficient

Note: We could have also worked with the distances covered by B and equated that difference to 2

The correct answer is option C.

115. Let the distance be d miles.

Let the normal speed of the man be n miles per hour.

Thus, normal time = $\left(\dfrac{d}{n}\right)$ hours.

From statement 1:

New speed = $(n + 6)$ miles per hour.

Thus, new time = $\left(\dfrac{d}{n + 6}\right)$ hours.

Since the new time is 1 hour less than previous, we have:

$$\frac{d}{n} - \frac{d}{n+6} = 1$$

$$=> \frac{6d}{n(n+6)} = 1$$

$$=> \frac{n(n+6)}{6} = d \dots (i)$$

However, the value of $\left(\frac{d}{n}\right)$ cannot be determined since the individual values of d and n cannot be determined. – Insufficient

From statement 2:

New speed = $(n-4)$ miles per hour.

Thus, new time = $\left(\frac{d}{n-4}\right)$ hours.

Since the new time is 1 hour more than previous, we have:

$$\frac{d}{n-4} - \frac{d}{n} = 1$$

$$=> \frac{4d}{n(n-4)} = 1$$

$$=> \frac{n(n-4)}{4} = d \dots (ii)$$

However, the value of $\left(\frac{d}{n}\right)$ cannot be determined since the individual values of d and n cannot be determined. – Insufficient

Thus, from (i) and (ii) together:

$$\frac{n(n+6)}{6} = \frac{n(n-4)}{4}$$

$$=> 2n^2 + 12n = 3n^2 - 12n => n^2 = 24n$$

$$=> n = 24$$

Thus, from (i):

$$d = \frac{24 \times 30}{6} = 120$$

$$=> \frac{d}{n} = \frac{120}{24} = 5 \text{ - Sufficient}$$

The correct answer is option C.

116. From statement 1:

We know that:

Distance between points Q and R = 500 meters.

Distance between points P and R

= (Distance between points P and Q) + (Distance between points Q and R)

= 100 + 500 = 600 meters.

Thus, A will travel 600m , while B will travel 500m.

However, there is no information about the speeds of A and B. – Insufficient

From statement 2:

The distance between the points P and R or the points Q and R is not known. – Insufficient

Thus, from both statements together:

We know that if A had started from Q and B had started from P, then A would have reached R earlier than B.

Distance travelled by A = Distance between points Q and R = 500 meters

Since B, having started from P, would have been 100 meters behind A, we have:

Distance travelled by B =

(Distance between points P and R) – 100

= 600 – 100 = 500 meters.

Thus, we see that A covers 500 meters in the same time as B covers 500 meters.

Thus, the speeds of A and B are the same.

Thus, in the original situation, since A starts 100 meters behind B, A would not reach R before B.

The answer to the question is 'No'. – Sufficient

The correct answer is option C.

117. From statement 1:

We know that:

The distance, in miles, travelled by the spaceship in the kth second is given by $(30k^2 - 5)$, where k is a positive integer.

Thus, we have:

- $k = 1$: Distance travelled in the 1st second = $30 \times 1^2 - 5 = 25$ miles

- $k = 2$: Distance travelled in the 2nd second = $30 \times 2^2 - 5 = 115$ miles

- $k = 3$: Distance travelled in the 3rd second = $30 \times 3^2 - 5 = 265$ miles

- $k = 4$: Distance travelled in the 4th second = $30 \times 4^2 - 5 = 475$ miles

- $k = 5$: Distance travelled in the 5th second = $30 \times 5^2 - 5 = 745$ miles

Thus, total distance travelled by the spaceship in 5 seconds

= 25 + 115 + 265 + 475 + 745

= 1625 miles

Since average speed is the ratio of total distance to total time, we have:

Average speed = $\dfrac{1625}{5}$ = 325 miles per second. – Sufficient

From statement 2:

We know that:

The total distance, in miles, travelled by the spaceship in k seconds is given by $5k^2 (2k + 3)$, where k is a positive integer.

Thus, the total distance travelled in 5 seconds

= $5 \times 5^2 \times (2 \times 5 + 3) = 125 \times 13$

= 1625 miles

This is the same as obtained from Statement 1. – Sufficient

The correct answer is option D.

118. From statement 1:

The integers in set A as well as that in set B form an 'Arithmetic Progression'.

Thus, the average of the integers in either set is simply the average of the first term and the last term.

Since each set consists of consecutive even integers, the difference between any two consecutive integers in either set is '2'.

In an Arithmetic Progression having the first term as x and constant difference between consecutive terms as d, the kth term is given by $\{x + d\,(k - 1)\}$.

Thus, we have:

- For set A:

  First term = a

  Last term = $a + (n - 1) \times 2$

  Thus, the average of the integers in the set A
  $$= \left\{ \frac{a + (a + 2\,(n - 1))}{2} \right\} = \left\{ \frac{2a + 2\,(n - 1)}{2} \right\} = a + n - 1$$

- For set B:

  First term = $a + 2n$

  Last term = $(a + 2n) + (n - 1) \times 2$

  Thus, the average of the integers in the set B
  $$= \left\{ \frac{(a + 2n) + (a + 2n + 2\,(n - 1))}{2} \right\} = \left\{ \frac{2a + 4n + 2\,(n - 1)}{2} \right\} = a + 3n - 1$$

Since the difference between the above means is 40, we have:

$(a + 3n - 1) - (a + n - 1) = 40$

$=> n = 20$ – Sufficient

From statement 2:

In the same manner as shown above, we have:

- Average of the integers in the set $A = (a + n - 1)$

- Average of the integers in the set $B = (a + 3n - 1)$

Since the sum of the above means is 120, we have:

$(a + 3n - 1) + (a + n - 1) = 120$

Since the value of a is not known, the value of n cannot be determined. – Insufficient

The correct answer is option A.

119. We know that:

Pipes A and B can fill the tank in 12 hours and 8 hours, respectively.

Thus, part of the tank filled by A and B in 1 hour = $\frac{1}{12}$ and $\frac{1}{8}$, respectively.

Let pipe C was opened x hours after pipes A and B were opened.

Let us assume that pipe C can empty the full tank in c hours.

Thus, part of the tank emptied by pipe C in 1 hour = $\frac{1}{c}$

We need to determine the value of c.

From statement 1:

We know that:

Three hours after pipes A and B were opened, the tank was only half filled.

Assuming that only A and B were open for these 3 hours ($x > 3$), total part of the tank filled by both

$= \left(\frac{1}{12} + \frac{1}{8}\right) \times 3 = \frac{5}{8} > \frac{1}{2}$

Thus, it implies that pipe C was also open for at least a part of these 3 hours since it would drain out some water and make the tank only half full, i.e. $x < 3$.

Since C was opened x hours after A and B were opened, out of the 3 hours, C was open for $(3 - x)$ hours.

Thus, part of the tank emptied by pipe C in $(3 - x)$ hours = $\frac{(3 - x)}{c}$

Thus, we have:

$\left(\frac{1}{12} + \frac{1}{8}\right) \times 3 - \frac{(3 - x)}{c} = \frac{1}{2}$

$=> \frac{3 - x}{c} = \frac{5}{8} - \frac{1}{2} = \frac{1}{8} \dots \text{(i)}$

Since the value of c is unknown, the value of x cannot be determined. – Insufficient

From statement 2:

The value of c cannot be determined only knowing that x is an integer. – Insufficient

Thus, from both statements together:

We have:

$$\frac{3 - x}{c} = \frac{1}{8}$$

$$=> c = 8\,(3 - x)$$

Since x is an integer, c must also be an integer.

Since $(3 - x)$ represents the number of hours for which C was working, it must be a positive quantity.

Thus, the possible values of x can be 1 or 2:

- $x = 1$: $c = 8\,(3 - 1) = 16$

- $x = 2$: $c = 8\,(3 - 2) = 8$

Thus, the value of c cannot be uniquely determined. – Insufficient

The correct answer is option E.

120.   From statement 1:

There is no information about the final average age of the students in the class or the number of students in the class. – Insufficient

From statement 2:

There is no information about the final average age of the students in the class or the average age of the students who join the class. – Insufficient

Thus, from statements 1 and 2 together:

Let the strength of the class before the students join = x.

Since the strength of the class after the students join increases by 50%, the number of students who join the class

= 50% of x

$= \dfrac{x}{2}$

Let the initial average age of the class = a years.

The average age of the students who join the class is 17 years.

The average age of all the students after the new students join = $(a - 1)$ years.

Thus, we have:

$$\dfrac{\left(x \times a + \dfrac{x}{2} \times 17\right)}{\left(x + \dfrac{x}{2}\right)} = a - 1$$

$$=> \dfrac{x\left(a + \dfrac{17}{2}\right)}{x\left(\dfrac{3}{2}\right)} = a - 1$$

$$=> a + \dfrac{17}{2} = \dfrac{3a}{2} - \dfrac{3}{2}$$

$$=> \dfrac{a}{2} = 10$$

$$=> a = 20 - \text{Sufficient}$$

The correct answer is option C.

121. Let the number of tests taken by Bob before taking the last two tests = x.

From statement 1:

We have no information about the average marks after taking the last two tests. – Insufficient

From statement 2:

We have no information about the average marks before taking the last two tests. – Insufficient

Thus, from statements 1 and 2 together:

Total marks obtained by Bob before taking the last two tests = $85x$.

Total marks obtained by Bob after taking the last two tests = $81(x + 2)$.

Thus, total marks scored by Bob in the last two tests

$= 81 (x + 2) - 85x$

$= 162 - 4x$

Since x (the number of tests taken) is a positive integer, we have: $x \geq 1$

$=> 162 - 4x \leq 158$

Thus, Bob scored at most 158 marks in his last 2 tests.

Thus, Bob's average marks in his last 2 tests is at most $\dfrac{158}{2} = 79$. – Sufficient

The correct answer is option C.

122. Let the average of the group of people be x years.

Let the number of people in the group initially be n.

From statement 1:

Total age of the people in the group initially $= nx$.

When 4 people with average age 40 years join, the new total age of the group of $(n + 4)$ people $= nx + 40 \times 4$

$= (nx + 160)$ years

Thus, average age of this group

$= \left(\dfrac{nx + 160}{n + 4} \right)$ years

This new average is 2 years more than the initial average. Thus, we have:

$\left(\dfrac{nx + 160}{n + 4} \right) = x + 2$

$=> nx + 160 = (n + 4)(x + 2)$

$=> nx + 160 = nx + 4x + 2n + 8$

$=> 4x + 2n = 152$

$=> 2x + n = 76$

There are two unknowns in one equation and hence, we cannot determine whether $x \geq$ 20.

For example, we may have:

- $n = 20 => x = \dfrac{76-20}{2} = 28 \geq 20$ - Satisfies

- $n = 40 => x = \dfrac{76-40}{2} = 18 \not\geq 20$ - Does not satisfy

Thus, there is no unique answer. – Insufficient

From statement 2:

Total age of the people in the group initially = nx.

When 4 people with average age 40 years join, the new total age of the group of $(n+4)$ people = $nx + 40 \times 4$

= $(nx + 160)$ years

Thus, average age of this group

= $\left(\dfrac{nx+160}{n+4}\right)$ years

This new average is double the initial average. Thus, we have:

$\left(\dfrac{nx+160}{n+4}\right) = 2x \ldots \text{(ii)}$

$=> nx + 160 = 2nx + 8x$

$=> nx + 8x = 160$

$=> x(8 + n) = 160$

$=> x = \dfrac{160}{8+n}$

Since $\dfrac{160}{8} = 20$, and n is a positive integer, we must have:

$\dfrac{160}{8+n} < 20$

$=> x < 20$

Thus, the average age of the group initially was not at least 20. – Sufficient

The correct answer is option B.

123.   Total earnings of Martin in the first 5 years = $\$ (15000 \times 5) \ldots \text{(i)}$

We need to determine Martin's average annual earnings in the last 5 years.

Average annual earnings in the last 5 years = $\dfrac{\text{Total earnings in the last 5 years}}{5}$

Thus, we need to determine Martin's total annual earnings in the last 5 years.

From statement 1:

Total earnings of Martin in the first 25 years = $ (27000×25) ...(ii)

However, we cannot determine his total annual earnings in the last 5 years. – Insufficient

From statement 2:

Total earnings of Martin in the last 25 years = $ (34000×25) ...(iii)

Thus, from (i) and (iii):

His total earnings in 30 years = $ $(15000 \times 5 + 34000 \times 25)$ ...(iv)

However, we cannot determine his total annual earnings in the last 5 years. – Insufficient

Thus, from statements 1 and 2 together:

From (ii) and (iv):

His total annual earnings in the last 5 years

= (His total earnings in 30 years) − (His earnings in the first 25 years)

= $\${(15000 \times 5 + 34000 \times 25) - (27000 \times 25)}$

= $ $(3000 \times 25 + 34000 \times 25 - 27000 \times 25)$

= $ (25×10000)

=> Average annual earnings in the last 5 years

=$ $\left(\dfrac{25 \times 10000}{5} \right)$ = $50000 – Sufficient

The correct answer is option C.

124. Let the number of examinees in the morning be x.

Thus, the number of examinees in the afternoon = $(50 - x)$.

From statement 1:

The average score for the examinees in the morning was 68.

Thus, total score of the examinees in the morning = $68x$.

However, since the score of the examinees in the afternoon and the number of examinees in the morning and afternoon is not known, the average score of all the examinees cannot be determined. – Insufficient

From statement 2:

The average score for the examinees in the afternoon was 74.

Thus, total score of the examinees in the morning $= 74 \times (50 - x)$.

However, since the score of the examinees in the morning and the number of examinees in the morning and afternoon is not known, the average score of all the examinees cannot be determined. – Insufficient

Thus, from statements 1 and 2 together:

Total score of all examinees

$= 68x + 74 \, (50 - x)$

$= 3700 - 6x$

Thus, the average score of all the examinees

$= \dfrac{3700 - 6x}{50}$

However, the value of x is unknown, hence, the answer cannot be determined. – Insufficient

The correct answer is option E.

Alternate approach:

Since the number of examinees in the morning and/or the afternoon is not known, we cannot determine the average of the entire group. – Insufficient

Note: Had the ratio of the number of examinees been know, say, $a : b$, the average could have been determined as:

Average of all examinees $= \left(\dfrac{68a + 74b}{a + b} \right)$

125. Let the number of terms in the list $= n$

Let the sum of the n terms $= S$

Thus, the average of the n terms $= \dfrac{S}{n}$

Thus, the required percent value

$$= \dfrac{\left(\dfrac{S}{n}\right)}{S} \times 100\%$$

$$= \dfrac{100}{n}\%$$

From statement 1:

$n = 8$

Thus, the required percent value

$$= \dfrac{100}{8}\%$$

$= 12.5\%$ – Sufficient

From statement 2:

The number of terms is not known. – Insufficient

The correct answer is option A.

126. The paths followed by Lisa and Paul are shown in the diagram below:

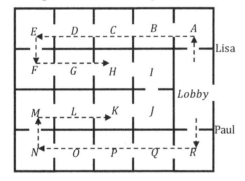

From statement 1:

Ratio of the times spent by Lisa and Paul in each room

$$= \dfrac{2x}{3x} = \dfrac{2}{3}$$

Thus, the ratio of the number of rooms covered by Lisa and Paul in the same time

$$= \dfrac{1}{\left(\dfrac{2}{3}\right)} = \dfrac{3}{2}$$

Total number of rooms = 18.

Thus, the number of rooms covered by Lisa $= \dfrac{3}{3+2} \times 18 = 10.8$, i.e. the 11th room.

Also, the number of rooms covered by Paul $= \dfrac{2}{3+2} \times 18 = 7.2$, i.e. the 8th room.

Thus, Lisa would have entered the 11th room, starting from room A i.e. room K and Paul would have entered the 8th room, starting from room R i.e. room K.

Thus, both would be in room K at the same time. – Sufficient

From statement 2:

We know that Lisa spends 10 minutes less time in each room than Paul does.

Let Paul spends x minutes in each room.

Thus, Lisa spends $(x - 10)$ minutes in each room.

Let us assume that when both meet, Paul and Lisa have covered p and l rooms, respectively.

Since the total number of rooms is 18, and both meet in a particular room, we have:

$p + l = 18 + 1 = 19$

$=> l = 19 - p \dots (i)$

Total time spent by Paul $= px$ minutes.

Total time spent by Lisa $= l(x - 10)$ minutes.

Since both have travelled for the same time we have:

$px = l(x - 10)$

Using relation (i):

$px = (19 - p)(x - 10)$

$=> px = 19x - px + 10p - 190$

$=> 2px = 19x + 10p - 190$

There are two unknowns in the above equation, hence the values of p and l cannot be determined. – Insufficient

The correct answer is option A.

127. From statement 1:

Total cost of the dinner

$= \$19k \ldots (i)$

However, the value of k is unknown. – Insufficient

From statement 2:

Total cost of the dinner

$= \$18\,(k+1) \ldots (ii)$

However, the value of k is unknown. – Insufficient

Thus, from statements 1 and 2 together:

From (i) and (ii), we have:

$19k = 18\,(k+1)$

$=> k = 18$

$=>$ Total cost of the dinner

$= \$19k$

$= \$\,(19 \times 18)$ – Sufficient

The correct answer is option C.

128. Total number of seats in the theatre $= 35 \times 27 = 945$

Thus, the number of seats occupied = Total number of seats – Number of seats unoccupied

From statement 1:

The total number of unoccupied seats in the front 20 rows $= 10 \times 20 = 200$

However, the total number of unoccupied seats in the remaining rows is not known.

– Insufficient

From statement 2:

The total number of unoccupied seats in the back 16 rows $= 20 \times 16 = 320$

However, the total number of unoccupied seats in the remaining rows is not known. –Insufficient

Thus, from statements 1 and 2 together:

The 20th row from the front is common to the front 20 rows as well as the back 16 rows.

Thus, the total number of unoccupied seats

= (Number of unoccupied seats in the front 20 rows) + (Number of unoccupied seats in the back 16 rows) – (Number of unoccupied seats in the 20th row from the front)

However, the number of unoccupied seats in the 20th row from the front is not known. – Insufficient

The correct answer is option E.

129. From statement 1:

Distance travelled = 90 miles.

Speed of car S = 50 miles per hour.

Thus, time taken by car S to cover the entire distance = $\dfrac{90}{50}$ = 1.8 hours.

Speed of car T = 45 miles per hour.

Thus, time taken by car T to cover the entire distance = $\dfrac{90}{45}$ = 2 hours.

Since information is given only about the speeds of the two cars, and not about the consumption of gasoline, the rate of consumption of gasoline cannot be determined. – Insufficient

From statement 2:

Gasoline consumed by car S for every 20 miles = 1 gallon.

Thus, gasoline consumed by car S for 90 miles = $\dfrac{90}{20}$ = 4.5 gallons.

Gasoline consumed by car T for every 30 miles = 1 gallon.

Thus, gasoline consumed by car T for 90 miles = $\dfrac{90}{30}$ = 3 gallons.

Since information is given only about the consumption of gasoline, and not about the time taken for the journey, the rate of consumption of gasoline cannot be determined. – Insufficient

Thus, from statements 1 and 2 together:

Time taken by car S = 1.8 hours.

Gasoline consumed by car S = 4.5 gallons.

Thus, rate of consumption of gasoline = $\dfrac{4.5}{1.8}$ = 2.5 gallons per hour.

Time taken by car T = 2 hours.

Gasoline consumed by car T = 3 gallons.

Thus, rate of consumption of gasoline = $\dfrac{3}{2}$ = 1.5 gallons per hour.

Thus, car S used more gasoline per hour than car T. – Sufficient

The correct answer is option C.

130. Average weight of the packages

$= \dfrac{\text{Total weight of the packages}}{\text{Number of packages}}$

From statement 1:

The number of packages is not known. – Insufficient

From statement 2:

The weights of the packages are not known. – Insufficient

Thus, from statements 1 and 2 together:

Total weight of the packages is greater than 14500 grams.

Number of packages is less than 25.

Let us work with the total weight as 14500 (least value) and the number of packages as 24 (greatest value):

Average weight of the packages

$= \dfrac{14500}{24}$

$= 604\dfrac{1}{6}$ grams, i.e. greater than 600 grams.

If the total weight is greater than 14500 and the number of packages is fewer than 24, the average weight would increase.

Thus, the average weight is greater than 600 grams. – Sufficient

The correct answer is option C.

131.   From statement 1:

$$\dfrac{w + x + y + z}{4} = n$$

$$\Rightarrow w + x + y + z = 4n$$

$$\Rightarrow (n - w) + (n - x) + (n - y) + (n - z) = 4n - (w + x + y + z)$$

$$= 4n - 4n$$

$$= 0 - \text{Sufficient}$$

From statement 2:

For any set of consecutive integers for w, x, y and z, the value of n would be unknown. – Insufficient

The correct answer is option A.

132.   From statement 1:

There is no information regarding the number of members in 1985 and 1995. – Insufficient

From statement 2:

There is no information regarding the contribution made in 1985 and 1995. – Insufficient

Thus, from statements 1 and 2 together:

Let the number of members in 1985 be n.

Thus, the number of members in 1995 $= 2n$.

Thus, average contribution in 1985 $= \$\left(\dfrac{505210}{n}\right)$

Average contribution in 1995 = $ $\left(\dfrac{1225890}{2n} \right)$

Thus, percent change in average contribution

$= \dfrac{\text{(Average contribution in 1995)} - \text{(Average contribution in 1985)}}{\text{(Average contribution in 1985)}} \times 100\%$

$= \left(\dfrac{\dfrac{1225890}{2n} - \dfrac{505210}{n}}{\dfrac{505210}{n}} \right) \times 100\%$

$= \left(\left(\dfrac{1225890 - 2 \times 505210}{2n} \right) \times \left(\dfrac{n}{505210} \right) \right) \times 100\%$

$= \left(\dfrac{1225890 - 2 \times 505210}{2 \times 505210} \right) \times 100\%$

Thus, the required percent change can be calculated. – Sufficient

(Note: The actual percent value is not required to be calculated)

The correct answer is option C.

133. Let the original average age of the class be a years and the strength of the class be n.

Thus, total age of all students = $n \times a$ years.

Let g be the number of students left the class and their average age was l years.

Thus, total age of the students who left the class = $g \times l$ years.

Thus, the final average age of the class of $(n - g)$ students = $(a - 2)$ years.

Thus, total age of the students remaining in the class = $(n - g)(a - 2)$ years.

Thus, equating the sum of ages of all the students, we have:

$na - gl = (n - g)(a - 2)$

$=> na - gl = na - ga - 2n + 2g$

$=> ga = g(l + 2) - 2n$

$=> a = l + 2 - \dfrac{2n}{g} \dots \text{(i)}$

We need to determine the value of $(a - 2)$

From statement 1:

$l = 22 \dots \text{(ii)}$

However, the value of a cannot be determined from (i) since the value of g is unknown. – Insufficient

From statement 2:

$$n - g = n\left(1 - \frac{40}{100}\right)$$

$$=> n - g = \frac{3}{5}n$$

$$=> \frac{2}{5}n = g$$

$$=> \frac{2n}{g} = 5 \ldots \text{(iii)}$$

Substituting (iii) in (i), we have:

$$a = l + 2 - \frac{2n}{g}$$

$$=> a = l + 2 - 5$$

$$=> a = l - 3 \ldots \text{(iv)}$$

However, the value of a cannot be determined since the value of l is unknown. – Insufficient

Thus, from statements 1 and 2 together:

From (ii) and (iv):

$$a = l - 3$$

$$=> a = 22 - 3 = 19$$

$$=> a - 2 = 17 \text{ – Sufficient}$$

The correct answer is option C.

Alternate approach:

Logically, we can proceed as follows:

From statement 1 and the main problem body, we only have information about the average age of the students who left and the difference in average age of the class; there is no information about the number of students. – Insufficient

From statement 2, we only have information about the number of students; there is no information about the average age. – Insufficient

From statements 1 and 2 together, we get all the necessary information. – Sufficient

134.   Total length of the race = 1000 meters.

Speed of A = 10 meters per second.

Thus, the time taken by A to complete the race

$$= \frac{\text{Distance}}{\text{Speed}}$$

$$= \frac{1000}{10}$$

= 100 seconds

From statement 1:

Since A beat B by 250m, distance covered by B when A completes 1000 meters

= 1000 – 250

= 750 meters

Thus, B covered 750 meters in 100 seconds (the time A took to complete the race).

Thus, speed of B

$$= \frac{750}{100}$$

= 7.5 meters per second – Sufficient

From statement 2:

Had A allowed B to start the race from a point 100 meters ahead of him, A would have still managed to beat B by 20 seconds.

Since A beats B by 20 seconds, time taken by B to complete the race of 900 meters (after a start of 100 meters allowed by A)

= 100 + 20

= 120 seconds

Thus, B travelled 900 meters in 120 seconds to complete the race.

Thus, speed of B

$$= \frac{900}{120}$$

= 7.5 meters per second – Sufficient

The correct answer is option D.

135.   Speed while going uphill = 6 miles per hour.

Let distance travelled uphill = u miles.

Thus, time taken to travel uphill = $\dfrac{u}{6}$ hours.

Speed while coming downhill = 10 miles per hour.

Let distance travelled downhill = d miles.

Thus, time taken to travel downhill = $\dfrac{d}{10}$ hours.

Total distance travelled = $(u + d)$ miles.

Total time taken = $\left(\dfrac{u}{6} + \dfrac{d}{10}\right)$ hours.

From statement 1:

Since the total trip took 5 hours, we have:

$$\dfrac{u}{6} + \dfrac{d}{10} = 5$$

$$=> 5u + 3d = 150 \ldots (i)$$

However, the value of u cannot be determined from the above equation since there are two unknowns. – Insufficient

From statement 2:

Since the average speed for the entire trip was 8 miles per hour, we have:

$$\text{Average speed} = \dfrac{\text{Total distance}}{\text{Total time}} = 8$$

$$=> \dfrac{(u + d)}{\left(\dfrac{u}{6} + \dfrac{d}{10}\right)} = 8$$

$$=> \dfrac{30\,(u + d)}{(5u + 3d)} = 8$$

$$=> 10u = 6d$$

$$=> d = \dfrac{5}{3}u \ldots (ii)$$

However, the value of u cannot be determined from the above equation since the value of d is unknown. – Insufficient

Thus, from statements 1 and 2 together:

Substituting the value of d from (ii) in (i):

$$5u + 3\left(\frac{5}{3}u\right) = 150$$

$$\Rightarrow u = 15 \text{ – Sufficient}$$

The correct answer is option C.

Alternate approach:

Since in this question, the average speed is the average of the two speeds $\left(8 = \frac{6 + 10}{2}\right)$, it implies that the time taken to go uphill must be the same as the time taken to come downhill.

Thus, time taken for each part of the trip $= \frac{5}{2}$ hours.

Thus, distance travelled uphill = Speed × Time $= 6 \times \frac{5}{2} = 15$ miles.

Chapter 6

Talk to Us

Have a Question?

Email your questions to info@manhattanreview.com and we would be happy to answer you. Your questions can be related to a concept, an application of a concept, an explanation of a question, a suggestion for an alternate approach, or anything else you wish to ask regarding the GMAT.

Please mention the page number when quoting from the book.

GMAC – Quant Resources

- *Official Guide*: It is the best resource to prepare for the GMAT. It is a complete GMAT book. It comes with a Diagnostic test, which helps you measure your capability beforehand. It features Verbal, Quantitative, and Integrated Reasoning questions types. The book contains an access code to avail GMATPrep Software, Online Question Bank and Exclusive Video.

- *GMATPrep Software*: If you buy the OG, you get a free online resource from the GMAC— the testmaker. Apart from practice questions and explanation, it also has two genuine Computer Adaptive tests; you can also buy four additional CATs and few practice questions upon the payment.

Best of luck!

Happy Learning!

Professor Dr. Joern Meissner
& The Manhattan Review Team

Manhattan Admissions

You are a unique candidate with unique experience.
We help you to sell your story to the admissions committee.

Manhattan Admissions is an educational consulting firm that guides academic candidates through the complex process of applying to the world's top educational programs. We work with applicants from around the world to ensure that they represent their personal advantages and strength well and get our clients admitted to the world's best business schools, graduate programs and colleges.

We will guide you through the whole admissions process:

- ☑ Personal Assessment and School Selection
- ☑ Definition of your Application Strategy
- ☑ Help in Structuring your Application Essays
- ☑ Unlimited Rounds of Improvement
- ☑ Letter of Recommendation Advice
- ☑ Interview Preparation and Mock Sessions
- ☑ Scholarship Consulting

To schedule a free 30-minute consulting and candidacy evaluation session or read more about our services, please visit or call:

 www.manhattanadmissions.com   +1.212.334.2500

Made in the USA
Las Vegas, NV
08 December 2021

36709858R00122